THE FLIGHT OF THE STORK

THE FLIGHT OF THE STORK

Anne C. Bernstein

DELACORTE PRESS / NEW YORK

Published by
Delacorte Press
1 Dag Hammarskjold Plaza
New York, New York 10017

Excerpts from Warren J. Gadpaille,
The Cycles of Sex, edited by Lucy Freeman
used by permission of Charles Scribner's Sons.

Manufactured in the United States of America

First printing

Designed by Leo McRee

Library of Congress Cataloging in Publication Data
Bernstein, Anne C   1944–
The flight of the stork.

Bibliography: p.
1. Sex instruction.   2.   Children's questions
and answers.   I.   Title.
HQ57.B49   612.6   77–15781

ISBN 0–440–02657–1

Acknowledgments

I would like to thank the people who helped make this book possible.

Philip A. Cowan first pointed out the need for a study of children's thinking about the origin of babies. His guidance throughout the original research was invaluable. Margaret T. Singer, Kenneth Craik, and Joseph Kuypers provided many helpful suggestions, and Sonne Lemke's work on children's identity concepts added an important dimension to the research.

The children I spoke with, and their parents, who consented to their children's being interviewed, were, of course, indispensable. The children, with their ingenuous and imaginative views and their eagerness to serve as consultants, made the work a pleasure. The Children's Community Center in Berkeley, California, the Early Childhood Education Department of Cabrillo College in Aptos, California, and Maria Pinedo of San Francisco all helped me to make connections with children and families.

Lonnie Garfield Barbach, Ernest Callenbach, Daniel Goldstine, Katherine Larner, and David Swanger provided encouragement and assistance in the critical juncture between completed thesis and prospective book.

Donald Rothman read the manuscript as I wrote it, keeping me attentive to questions of style and clarity. An innovative teacher of writing, he more than anyone else provided both support and criticism as the book was in progress. Betty Cohen, Martin Gold, Alan Graubard, and Diana Rothman made many excellent suggestions for revising the manuscript, and Mildred Ash shared her observations on the labeling of female sexual anatomy. Nancy Feinstein, Wendy Roberts, and Vicki Strang were valuable consultants.

ACKNOWLEDGMENTS

Rhoda Weyr, my agent, was a vital source of support, counsel, and savvy. Betty Kelly, my editor, gave me encouragement and artful help in shaping up chapters where they tended to sag.

I'm deeply grateful to you all.

—A.C.B.

For my mother and father

Contents

Preface

Storks fly through the air dangling babies from diaper slings. Cabbage patches are filled with infants hidden among the leaves. Doctors pull forth babies from black bags. The traditional child-tailored myths of creation are on the way out. Happily, few children are now being told these age-old parental lies, and fewer still believe them.

As part of my research at the University of California, Berkeley, I decided to find out what children understand of the explanations and gossip that form their early sex education. So I asked children their own perennial question: How do people get babies? And they told me.

It might seem as if the answer to that question will depend on what a child has been told, but that's not the case. Children continue to amaze the adults who have conscientiously imparted the "facts of life" with their own fantasized versions of these "facts." Even when adults give children straight facts, the story of human reproduction often gets twisted into a remarkable version of creation.

Jane, age four, told me: "To get a baby to grow in your tummy, you just make it first. You put some eyes on it. Put the head on, and hair, some hair, all curls. You make it with head stuff you find in the store that makes it for you. Well, the mommy and daddy make the baby and then they put it in the tummy and then it goes quickly out."

Jane had never been told that babies were manufactured, using parts purchased from the store. She put together the

answer out of information pieced together by a thread of
child logic that reflected her understanding of the physical
world.

How did I happen to be talking to Jane about how people
get babies? My interest in sex education began some years
back.

In 1948, I was four years old and my mother was pregnant. My parents "prepared" me for Andrew's birth by reading to me Marie Hall Ets's book, *The Story of a Baby*. It
soon became my favorite. I loved the story of the egg
"smaller than a seed of hay that flies like dust in the wind"
growing in its "house without windows or doors." I was
fascinated by the pictures of the wrinkled, tightly curled
embryos that changed from a curious squiggle on the page
to something that looked just like a baby.

In those days, I could not yet read, but I could remember.
I delighted in amazing adults by reciting word for word the
books I had heard most often, turning the pages at the appropriate time. For the "baby book," though, I wanted an
audience of children, since I was eager to share this wonderful story with my friends. I made the rounds of the
neighborhood, "reading" the book to all the kids. Years
later I learned that my educational campaign had caused
a flood of phone calls from the other mothers to mine: "Do
you know what your daughter is doing?!"

A few years after Andrew was born, I started lobbying
(in vain) for a sister. My mother seemed reluctant to come
right out and say that two children would do quite nicely
thank you. Instead, she rested her case on a statement of
fact: There was no baby growing inside her now. "Well," I
argued, "just tell Daddy to plant the seed." My brother,
playing nearby with a pail and shovel, came into the conversation, waving his shovel: "Me help Daddy plant the seed."
I knew that was silly. Although how the seed was planted
was still a mystery to me, I knew that it didn't take a shovel
and was nothing a three-year-old could do.

As a child, I wanted to learn about what adults thought

about having babies and what their sexual experiences were.
Later, as an adult, I turned to the study of children's ideas
of how people get babies. Early in my studies I took a class
with Professor Philip A. Cowan. I remember his saying that
there had been much speculation about how children think
about how people get babies, most of it based on adult
memories or projections about childhood. No one, however, had ever bothered to ask the children themselves.
Years later, when I was ready to begin my own research,
I knocked on his door and asked him, "Has anybody asked
them yet?" He said no, and I said, "Then I'm going to."

I talked with over a hundred children from three to twelve
years old. I asked them how people get babies, how mommies get to be mommies, and how daddies get to be daddies.
I asked them when mothers and fathers *start* to be mothers
and fathers, and called upon each child to explain how his
mother and father got to be *his* mother and father. I asked
what the word "born" means and what had happened at
the child's birth. All of the children I interviewed had at
least one younger brother or sister, and I asked each child
why his younger sibling had come to live at his house as
part of his family.

I asked the younger children: What if some people who
lived in a cave in the desert, where there weren't any other
people, wanted to have a baby. Because they had never
known any other people, they didn't know how people get
babies. What if they asked you for help? If they asked you
what they should do if they wanted a baby, what would you
tell them?

And to the older children, my question was: What did
you think about how people get babies before you understood it as well as you do now? What did you think when
you were little?

I approached each child as a consultant, asking his or her
help in my work, which I explained was learning how kids
think about some things. I emphasized that it was their way

of thinking, not the rightness or wrongness of their answers, that interested me. I did not provide the children with any information, nor did I introduce terms or concepts not mentioned by the children themselves. In speaking with over one hundred children, never did one turn the tables on me to ask me information about reproduction.

I use the ages of children in my examples only to help identify the children speaking. These ages are not intended as norms, or indications of how a child "should" think about reproduction at age four, seven, or eleven. The *sequence* of the levels which I will discuss should be the same for all children, but the ages at which they are reached may differ considerably. The children I talked with are not representative of the entire population. Most, but not all, are white and middle-class. They live in a fairly sophisticated region of the country (the San Francisco Bay Area), and they have received more direct teaching on this subject than most children have. While education does not determine the level of explanation children give to the question How do people get babies? repeated experience with ideas does have an influence. As a result, we can expect that the children described in this book are probably a little younger than most of the children whose thinking about the origin of babies theirs most resembles.

Parents should not become discouraged about their children's rate of development or attempt to push them to race up the "ladder" of developmental levels. Swiss psychologist Jean Piaget calls this desire to speed up the natural rhythms of children's learning "the American disease": racing to the end instead of enjoying the journey. Basic to his way of thinking about children's developing knowledge is that they cannot skip or leap over steps; each way of solving problems builds on the previous way. And each level of thinking about the origin of babies has its own delightful insights into the mind of a child.

The world has become so complex that many of us find ourselves awed by the responsibility of raising children when we cannot anticipate how accelerating change will transform the conditions they will live with as adults. Our grandparents did not question that they knew what they needed to be good parents. If they had any questions, they were confident that their own parents could provide the answers. Many of the adults I know best feel that our parents did not, and could not, prepare us for the world we now live in. We are unsure about how to equip our own children to live with change and to take control over change in order that they and the world may survive.

Such uncertainty about parenting has led to an unprecedented search for experts to tell us how: how to love, how to fight, how to like ourselves, and especially, because it is part of the way we ourselves can change the world, how to raise our children. There is nothing so revealing about the true dimensions of an expert than the discovery that others look to you for advice about how to live and trust important aspects of their children's future to your counsel. In writing a book that goes beyond describing children's thinking, to suggest "how to" talk with them, I have been humbled by the responsibility.

And so a word about "experts" and how to use the advice they have to offer. As you cut the suit to fit your body and not your body to fit the suit, so take expert advice only when it fits. If what I suggest goes against your grain, trust yourself. You'll be a better parent for it.

1

Children Think Differently from Adults

ALAN (AGE THREE): If Daddy put his egg in you, then I must be a chicken.

SUSAN (AGE FOUR): To get a baby, go to the store and buy a duck.

Every day, thousands of parents sit down to tell their children about the birds and the bees. And the cows. And the chickens. And the ducks. Parental descriptions of sex and birth often sound like morning roll call on Noah's ark. When it comes to people, however, the roll call becomes a lecture, taking on the precision of an advanced anatomy course, as the anxious parent rushes through enough detail to confuse a medical student.

Children take this information, process it through mental jungle gyms, and create their own versions of who comes from where, and how. The children seem content with their answers, and parents, having provided the answers, are not about to start following up with more questions. Chances are, therefore, that misunderstanding will persist.

The most effective way to tell children about sex is to provide information matched to their level of mental development. But because no one ever asks children what they really believe, as opposed to what they were told, we don't

understand how their ability to analyze and assimilate information changes year by year.

Do you remember what you thought as a child about how
people get babies? Take a few minutes to recollect what you
believed when you were four years old. Then close your
eyes and come up the years to age eight. How had your
understanding changed? By the time you were twelve, what
did you think?

In talking with groups of parents and psychology stu-
dents, I asked them to think themselves back to childhood
and share their beliefs about procreation. Many find this a
difficult thing to do. They find they cannot remember what
their child selves believed about sex and birth. Others remember only what they were told by their parents.

One man of about thirty recalled his father explaining
how you know the baby is coming long before it actually
arrives. He said getting a baby was very much like going to
a bakery: You go to the hospital and get a number; when
your number is called, you return to collect your baby.

A woman remembered believing that to get a baby you
put in a purchase order at the hospital. She had figured
this out for herself and believed it until she was eleven. To
put this story together, she drew on her own experience. Her
father had shown her the hospital where she and her brothers
and sisters were born, pointing it out to her as "the place
we got all you kids." Throughout her childhood she had
seen him handle countless purchase orders, since he ran
his business from their home, so it was only logical that he
had sent out a purchase order for them.

A woman remembered believing that a string goes from
the father to the mother during lovemaking, and it is this
string that impregnates her.

A man recalled his boyhood belief that intercourse was
like urination and took place standing up.

A woman remembered thinking that birth occurred when
the baby turned the knob of a little door in the sleeping
mother's back and walked out.

An older European woman told of her fright when, having missed a period as a teenager, she was convinced that a man had impregnated her while gallantly kissing her hand.

Perhaps your memories, like these people's, are very different from your current beliefs. Perhaps you cannot remember thinking any other way than you do now. It is hard to remember that you used to reason completely differently from the way you do now. The difficulty of translating thoughts from child logic to adult logic may block the road to memory.

This book is about some of the ways that children think differently from adults. In reading these pages, adults can learn to translate some of what they know into child logic so that they may communicate better with their children. By talking with children about how people get babies, I have gathered a collection of amusing stories which beautifully illustrate the way children think. The "out of the mouths of babes" quality of many of them is touching, and the adult who listens carefully has a lot to learn.

Many parents still find it difficult to talk about reproduction with their children. Their own emotional discomfort in talking about sex is one stumbling block, and their lack of information about what the child is really asking and is likely to understand is another. I will try to present a systematic description and explanation of the ways in which children are likely to embellish fact with fable at different ages. Knowing the direction in which your children's thinking is developing can help you present information in the way they can most readily absorb. I have divided children's explanations of the origins of babies into their six levels of problem-solving ability. In Chapters 3 through 8, I will present each level: the children's ideas about how people get babies, how their theories of reproduction tie in with their ideas about other of life's puzzles, and how parents can use this insight into children's thinking to communicate more effectively with their children.

The idea that children's thinking develops through a series

of levels is based on the work of Jean Piaget. Piaget regards each child as a philosopher who works at making the universe intelligible. Children ask themselves and others: What makes it night? What is a dream? How do people get babies? In growing up, children attempt to piece together answers to these and other questions, to explain to themselves the whats and hows and whys of the events that surround and involve them. They use all the resources at their disposal: what they themselves perceive with their senses, the information given them by others, and their own style of putting the puzzle together. As children develop, they shape the world in terms of their own level of understanding and then restructure their understanding when they take in information that doesn't fit into their old view of the universe. It is this structuring, restructuring, and eventual understanding that we are going to be talking about.

Piaget believes that the maturation of the nervous system and the muscular system plays a role in development, but it does not steal the show. He believes that the effect of the environment is important, but the child does not sit back passively and wait to be shaped by the outside world. Instead, Piaget emphasizes, from infancy onward the child actively seeks contact with the environment, looking for new levels of stimulation. When an event occurs, it is not merely registered as a "copy" of reality, but is interpreted and assigned meaning by the child. A blanket is not a blanket is not a blanket. To one child a blanket is something to suck, to another something to hide under while playing peek-a-boo, to a third it provides warmth during sleep, and to yet another it is a source of security and good feeling to cling to when alone.

How then does the child actively move from one stage of thinking to another? As we have already noted, maturation is necessary for development, but it is not enough. The child's intellect must also interact with the world around her. Only when the external world clashes with concepts already established in her mind is the child forced to modify these concepts and develop intellectually. Piaget describes this movement from stage to stage as resulting from the interaction of three different processes: assimilation (taking in), accommodation (putting out), and equilibration (balancing).

Each stage or level represents a general approach to understanding experience. These different modes of thinking form a fixed sequence. Each child must move from one to the next in the same order. No child goes from one level to another at random. Cultural and individual differences may speed up, slow down, or even stop development, so that all children of the same age are not at the same level, but the order of the levels each child must move through stays the same. I would like to remind the reader that the ages given for each level are not standards of "normality." Nor are they measures of general intellectual development. They serve only to describe the children I talked with whose thinking is described by that level. To compare your children to those quoted here in order to see how they "measure up" is to do them a disservice.

Because children are not miniature adults, they will not think like adults until they are themselves grown up. No matter how carefully a parent explains things, a child will misunderstand some part of the explanation, sometimes at the time, sometimes later. So, you might ask, why put the extra effort into answering questions with the child's thinking in mind? Why correct confusions that growing up will straighten out anyhow?

Perhaps the most important reason is that children ask their parents sincere questions and want and deserve truthful answers. Not the whole truth all at once, but as much of the truth as they request. It is not necessary to reel off explanations with all the details of a physiology text. It is important to find out what the child wants to know, and to do your best to satisfy his or her curiosity. Children know when their parents are being evasive, and they begin to wonder: Am I asking something I shouldn't? Is this some-

thing bad to think about? and Is there something wrong
with me for asking? They then quickly learn that if they
really want to find out about something, they must go somewhere else for the answers. But children also can sense
when their parents are responsive, aware of their needs,
and want to inform them. They learn that they can find out
what they want to know at home and can rely on their
parents as trustworthy sources of knowledge. When they
feel assured that the channels of communication are open,
they can pace their questions to their need to know, asking
one question now and waiting to mull over new ideas before
coming back to ask for more.

Another reason to encourage children's natural curiosity
about birth is that this curiosity is the starting point for
their interest in other questions of origin, the first step toward
thinking about cause and effect. Both Freud and Piaget agree
that children's inquiries into the origins of babies make up
an important step in their intellectual development. Freud
calls it "the first of the great problems of life." Piaget says,
"It is true that there will be children who ask questions
about origins before they ask them about birth but even
here the question arises whether it is not an interest in birth
which, thwarted and projected, is not at the root of these
questions about origin." He goes to say that "children's
ideas on the birth of babies follow the same laws as their
ideas in general." We will explore those ideas throughout
this book. For now, it is important to note that children's
questions about procreation are an early foray in their search
for knowledge. Encouraging the child's unguarded questions
and answering responsively also encourages the child as an
active, inquisitive explorer of the world.

Contrary to the old saw, what you don't know *can* hurt
you. Like the little boy who said, "If Daddy put his egg
in you then I must be a chicken," children who cannot distinguish between ova, the human eggs that grow babies, and
the eggs we eat for breakfast have occasion for worry. What
if instead of being born they had been eaten? Imagining

people as cannibals of their unborn young is disturbing. The child may refuse to eat eggs, or may eat them obediently and then feel queasy.

A six-and-a-half-year-old girl told her mother: "When I grow up, I'm not getting a daddy. And if I get a baby, I'm not going to let it out." Her belief that a baby could grow inside her body without her doing anything to set that process in motion leads to other upsetting thoughts. The idea of a baby inside who will never see the light of day, the feelings of this reluctant mother turned jailor who must keep the baby locked within her body, must no doubt cause her a great deal of worry and unhappiness. How relieved she would be to understand that if she didn't "get a daddy" no baby would begin to grow.

Among older children, vagueness and confusion about the mechanics of reproduction can lead to worry about pregnancy. Perhaps the child believes a kiss can impregnate. Or, uncertain about how the sperm gets to the egg, the child may become uncomfortable simply standing close to someone of the other sex. Adult women told me of their childhood fears that toilet seats and school benches, crowded buses and subways, might expose them to the risk of unwanted pregnancy.

Misconceptions about how people get babies can lead to conception in adolescence. Margaret Mead (who did not become pregnant until she was nearly forty) remembers her girlhood beliefs in *Blackberry Winter*: "The father's role in conception was essentially a feeding role, for many acts of intercourse were believed to be necessary to build up the baby, which was compounded of father's semen and mother's blood."

Misunderstanding can cause worry and psychological upset. Mary Jane Sherfey, in her book *The Nature and Evolution of Female Sexuality*, remembers a troubled ritual of her early adolescence. When she was twelve years old, her second-best girlfriend (whose uncle was a doctor and should know) told her that menstrual flow was really the remains of a dead baby. If you had sex, her girlfriend continued, the baby was fertilized and you got pregnant. If not, the baby died, and the menses were all that was left. She did not doubt this explanation, and it worried her.

> Most questions were ultimately answered simply, "God made us that way." Sad. All those dead babies! It seemed so cruel and even more so that I had to catch the few remains of my own dead baby month after month on an absorbent napkin and flush him down the toilet. I also decided that there was something wrong about God's attitude toward women. After all, He created the baby in me in the first place, and He must realize that I was forbidden to have sex and fertilize the baby until I was married (or much older). So He made the baby and then murdered it—all inside me!

On one occasion, she ritualized her grief and feelings of loss. Carefully, she wrapped her used sanitary napkins in Christmas wrapping paper, collected them in a painted shoebox, and buried them in her back yard. Solemnly she recited the Lord's Prayer and the Twenty-third Psalm over the tiny grave, saying "Good-bye, little baby."

Many misunderstandings are harmless and easily outgrown. Others become lingering concerns. Recalled by an adult who has made the transition to untroubled maturity, they make a good story. But the child who is experiencing the worry of misconstrued realities would prefer relief now to entertaining tales later.

Sympathetic, understanding adults can help reduce the child's confusion. When children learn that their parents are open and informative about answering their questions and discussing their concerns, they have available a trusted resource to turn to in times of confusion or worry. Parents' comfort and responsiveness in talking about sex and reproduction are important prerequisites to minimizing misunderstanding. Attitude provides the ground on which effective communication can be built. Knowing how children think at different developmental stages, what concepts are likely to be difficult for them and how, helps parents to build their educational efforts on a solid foundation.

Few of the parents of the children I questioned about reproduction had accurate ideas about the extent of their children's sexual knowledge. Parents of children at the lowest and highest levels of understanding predicted their offspring's answers with some accuracy. Most others assumed that their children knew a great deal more than they actually did. Many parents whose children produced fantastic versions of creation assumed that their children knew "the truth," and none anticipated the distortions that turned up.

As I talked to children of various ages, it became apparent that our present efforts at sex education often confuse children. A four-year-old boy, trying to explain how people get babies, told me, "First they were little, a duck, then they grow older into a baby." His solution seemed peculiar, but his source became clear when a four-year-old girl elaborated on a similar explanation. This little girl was explicit:

ME: How would a lady get a baby to grow in her tummy?

SUSAN: Get a duck. 'Cause one day I saw a book about them, and they just get a duck or a goose and they get a little more growned and then they turn into a baby.

ME: A duck will turn into a baby?

SUSAN: They give them some food, people food, and they grow like a baby. To get a baby, go to a store and buy a duck.

ME: How did you find that out?

SUSAN: I just saw, find out from this book.

Notice how literally Susan takes the idea popularized in folk wisdom. You are what you eat. A more important source of her confusion lies in the way many writers prepare books about sex and birth for children. One widely distributed book, which is recommended for children as young as three, starts with a pencil dot (to represent an ovum), then proceeds through the sex life of flowers, bees, rabbits, giraffes, chickens, and dogs before it reaches the human level. The evolutionary approach also reveals the hidden bias that sex is really an animal activity which can best be understood by watching animals. If we, like Pythagoras, were explaining the transmigration of the soul, then all the animals might make sense. As it is, few young children can encounter this kind of explanation without complete confusion.

Another writer, Selma Fraiberg, discovered a four-year-old boy who knew a sex-education book by heart, but insisted that some of the woman's eggs never become babies because the daddy eats them up. "It says so in my book," he claimed, and indeed it did—in a discussion of reproduction in fish.

Both of these examples show that confusion is likely to occur when several species are included in the same introductory book. When unable to figure out a certain aspect of human reproduction, the child extrapolates details from other sections of the book. These details seem no more fantastic to him in their adopted contexts than they were as originally stated. If there was a duck on page 4 and no human baby appeared until page 10, the child searching for an explanation of how that baby comes to be might mistake the layout sequence of the book for a causal sequence in the development of the baby. Before there was a baby, there was a duck!

Other studies suggest a way out of confusion. The experience of researchers into how children think about other concepts has shown that children can expand their understanding to include ways of reasoning one level more complex than their own. Using this idea as a guide, we can reduce sex misunderstanding to a minimum.

This book presents six stages in the development of children's thinking about how people get babies. Knowing the direction in which your children's thinking is developing can help you to present information in a way that they can most readily absorb.

2

Talking with Your Child about Sex and Birth

Although children's thinking and intellectual interest in the origin of babies will be our focus, I want to avoid the all-too-common educational practice of separating sex from reproduction, emotion from physiology, personal relationship from mechanics. Too frequently, sex education is limited to diagrams and procedures, a problem in human engineering amenable to technical solutions.

But learning and knowing cannot be isolated from feeling. How I feel about myself, how I feel about my teacher, and how I feel about what I am learning all affect whether that learning will be difficult or effortless, compartmentalized or usable in other contexts.

Many educators now recognize that their classrooms are filled with feeling children, not just problem-solvers or fact-memorizers. The move toward what George Isaac Brown has called "confluent education" is an important step toward facilitating learning. If reading, writing, and 'rithmetic skills bloom or wither depending on the emotional climate, how much more must the impact of sex education be influenced by its roots in feeling?

Only death seems to provoke the same level of discomfort most of us feel in talking about sex. Even those of us who feel some ease in talking with other adults about sex suddenly get cold feet when it's time to talk with children. Perhaps our awareness of the negative messages about sex we ourselves received as children reminds us that we need to be careful not to pass on our conflicts. Lacking real-life models for how to talk more openly with children, it is not easy to put our good intentions into action.

Whatever our feelings about sex are, we cannot avoid communicating them to our children. In addition to the verbal messages we are aware of sending, there are layers of simultaneously broadcast signals that qualify what we are trying to say. Tone of voice, inflection, facial expression, and gesture all communicate how we feel about what we are saying. Parents who tell their child that it is all right for her to masturbate, their voices flat and controlled, are giving her a double message. Their words say one thing, but the way they say it lets her know that on a deeper level they believe just the opposite. She cannot help but feel that she is doing something wrong, but because they do not acknowledge the nonverbal message, she is left confused about why she feels as she does.

Parents who evade issues, changing the subject when a question is asked or distracting the child when his behavior becomes overtly sexual, are also communicating their feelings to the child. No answer is also an answer. The message is clear if not explicit: This is something we don't talk about in this house; You are asking me improper questions I don't want to hear. The child learns that there is something wrong with him, feels embarrassed, and remains ignorant or seeks answers from friends who may know less but don't make him feel ashamed.

In *Between Marriage and Divorce*, Susan Braudy gives an example of how powerful nonverbal messages can be, leading to firmly held, but erroneous, convictions. Growing up, she never discussed either sex or religion with her mother. Instead, "my mother handed me a series of illustrated booklets about sex, when I was twelve. She had her 'I'm uneasy so don't ask' look on her face. When I was eight and asked her if she believed in God, she got that strained look on her face and told me that it was her private business. Once I found a tampax and asked her what it was. She got the same look on her face and said nothing. So that's why I knew tampax had something to do with religion."

While reading a book cannot provide an instant solution, the more aware we can become about our sexual values and feelings, the more informed we are on the issues, the better able we will be to teach our children about sex in an open, loving, and supportive way.

Any exchange between two people makes a statement about their relationship. A child who asks you "How do you go about having a baby?" or "Does it hurt when the sperm hits the egg?" is telling you that you are someone he trusts to give him reliable information without making him feel bad for wanting to know. Direct, honest responses to children's sexual curiosity give them both needed information and validation that they are good people, whose explorations of life, pleasure, and love are a valuable part of their development.

There is no way for parents to totally control the sex education of their children. I doubt whether it was ever possible, but in today's "global village" of rapid communications media, no child exposed to the light of day can be insulated from messages about sex. Not being able to control the whole show should not, however, discourage parents from assuming leading roles in the drama. Amid the clamor of competing claims to children's attention on sexual matters, there need to be reliable and loving people on whom they can depend through their years of growth. No matter what others say, they need to know what their parents think and feel about the things they are learning and feeling. Parents who establish themselves early in their children's lives as open and comfortable in dealing with sexuality will find that when their children have questions or worries to be cleared up, they will turn to their parents.

Teaching about sexuality begins at birth. The touching and handling and caressing loving parents provide in the course of infant care is essential to the newborn's survival

and development. Gentle, loving touch teaches infants to
relate warmly to others, while touch deprivation leads to
emotional and physical problems. Studies of infants in or-
phanages who were fed and kept clean but deprived of
adequate cuddling show how important the stimulation of
skin contact can be. The institutionalized children became
depressed, and their developing speech, motor coordination,
and relations with others were retarded or arrested. Colds
and common childhood diseases were fatal in a surprising
number of cases. (Gadpaille.)

This early stimulation between parent and child, so essential for the infant's survival and growth and so different from
the genital eroticism of sexually mature adults, is nonetheless
sexual. Sensual pleasure, the exchange of affection, physical
closeness leading to emotional intimacy, all are there.
Through early experiences of skin touching skin, infants
learn whether the life of the body and physical contact with
others yields pleasure or discomfort, reassurance or rejection.

It is with their parents that children first experience love,
both giving and receiving, so by loving children you are
providing sex education, too. (Pomeroy.) Children value
themselves when they feel valued by the people they most
love, the people on whom they know their survival rests:
their parents. From their parents, children learn either "I
am a lovable person whom others will care for" or "I am
unlovable and must protect myself from caring too much
for anyone."

The young child values his waste products as part of his
body. If he is made to feel that his bowel movement or urine
is bad, he may internalize these attitudes, and start to feel
that he himself is bad. Similarly, children who discover that
the genitals that give them pleasure cause disgust in their
parents will often feel that their genitals are bad, their feelings are wrong, and they are unworthy as people. (Fraiberg.)

Long before children enter school, their gender identity
and feelings about sexuality have been shaped by early
experiences with family members. Feeling good about one's

sexual identity is an important part of self-esteem. To like the fact of one's own sex, one must feel good about one's genitals. It is hard for a child to feel good about himself if his parents would have preferred him to have been put together differently.

In learning about sex differences, children learn both facts and values. Listening to the answers to their questions about genital differences, they pick up attitudes as well as information. Once they can move around well enough to observe others' bodies, have a social setting such as a nursery-school bathroom that permits repeated opportunities for looking, and have the mental ability to make comparisons, children will explore this intriguing discovery.

Until they see evidence to the contrary, both sexes assume that everybody is "just like me." Seeing the body of a naked child of the other sex will stimulate questions about why there's a difference. Boys may ask, "Where's her penis?" or "Why doesn't she have one, too?" or "What happened to it?" From girls, the questions may be "What is that?" or "Why does he have that?" or "What happened to mine?" Warren Gadpaille, who argues that the theory of "penis envy has been grossly misused as a basis for a thoroughly mistaken and derogatory theory of female inferiority," points out that these questions are most frequently asked "with strong curiosity but with little or no anxiety."

Unless complicated by negative attitudes toward the little girl's sexuality, penis envy is frequent but harmless. "Every parent has observed," writes Gadpaille, "and certainly every child 'knows,' that having something is preferable to not having it . . . On this basis alone, penis envy is both understandable and transient." Teaching more about other sex differences is often useful when children first begin to ask questions about genitals. The development of breasts or facial hair, changes in the size of genitals with maturation, and the presence of the female's internal organs round out the picture so that each sex is defined by what it has rather than by what it lacks. It is difficult for the girl, as well as the boy, to ask questions about something they cannot see. But both need to understand that they are specially designed, "on purpose," to be different so that they can make babies together when they are grown up.

One part of teaching is labeling. Middle-class Americans have tended to teach their children that a boy has a penis and a girl has a vagina. While clearly preferable to referring to genitals with a nonspecific "down there," the word *vagina* is usually used inaccurately to refer to the female external genitals, the vulva. Until recently, the clitoris was entirely ignored by parents teaching body parts to children, leaving their daughters to discover for themselves this unlabeled part that exists only to provide pleasure.

There is no way to satisfactorily teach female anatomy if a direct equivalence must be made to the male. Alix Shulman attempts to redress past grievances by introducing new terms and concepts to the dialogue between parent and child:

BOY: What's the difference between boys and girls?

MOTHER: Mainly their sex organs. A boy has a penis and a girl has a clitoris.

BOY: What's a clitoris?

MOTHER: It's a tiny sensitive organ on a girl's body about where a penis is on a boy's body. It feels good to touch, like your penis . . .

BOY: What's it for?

MOTHER: For making love, for pleasure. When people love each other, one of the ways they show it is by caressing one another's bodies, including their sex organs.

BOY: How do girls pee?

MOTHER: There's an opening below the clitoris for peeing. A man uses his penis for peeing, for making love, and for starting babies. Women have three separate places for these (and so on. . . .)

There is a great deal to applaud in this approach: using the child's curiosity as a guide in providing information; giving simple, direct answers that make the lesson a dialogue instead of a lecture; recognizing the importance of teaching boys as well as girls about female anatomy; and including talk about pleasure and lovemaking in discussing sex with children. But her comparisons are not wholly accurate. Women do not have two separate places for lovemaking and starting babies. Women and men make love with their whole bodies. While the clitoris is uniquely designed for pleasure, women's sexual preferences, as well as their patterns of genital nerve endings, do vary. We should not banish the vagina from the arena of love and pleasure to make up for the prior exclusion of the clitoris.

Children learn about sexuality as they are taught about sex differences and reproduction. For better or for worse. Rebecca Black, a San Francisco sex therapist, describes in these terms the double message parents too frequently communicate to their children: "Sex is dirty—save it for someone you love." Gadpaille urges, and I with him, "that nothing be taught to a child that he must subsequently unlearn for effective adulthood." Children taught that it is bad to pursue sexual pleasure often find it a difficult if not impossible task to convince themselves as adults that now at last it is good.

"The walls have ears," I remember groups of adults saying, drawing one another's attention to the fact that children were present, soaking up all that was said, things that were presumably over their heads. Children are observant. Noticing how adults treat each other and how they themselves are treated by adults, they are quick to catch the discrepancies between what we say and what we do, and are more deeply impressed by practice than by words. If they see that they themselves are treated with respect and are expected to be responsible to others, respecting their desires, they will come to value themselves and others, rejecting force or exploitation in their human relationships. By watching their parents' marriage, they learn how sexual intimates relate. Is the love between a woman and man mutually supportive, caring, tender, responsive, and responsible, or exploitative, critical, barren, and debasing? What they see at home as children will influence their expectations of what is possible for them when they become sexually active adults.

What a challenge. We cannot avoid communicating about sex to children. The way we relate to one another and how we talk about sexual differences, reproduction, and relationships all form a part of their sex education. How then can we guide them in their effort to integrate their sexuality into their lives as whole people when this is a task very much in progress for most of us? In order to help the children we love, we must first explore our own feelings about sexuality and become more comfortable with them. We know that a lot was lacking in our own sex education, and all of us still have some conflicts from time to time. To be clear with children we must first be clear with ourselves, recognizing that we have abilities and limits, and acknowledging our true values.

It is not always easy to talk about sex with children. Feeling ignorant is often a problem for parents. Nothing can impress us with how little we know more than a child wanting to know the hows and whys of things we have come to take for granted. How does a car work? Why does it rain? How come the sperm and the ovum have to get together to make a baby?

Luckily for most of us, you don't need to have every piece to the puzzle to get the picture across. It isn't necessary to understand all the complexities of sexual reproduction to teach your children what they want to know. Their learning, like our own, will continue throughout their lives. If you don't know the answer to a child's question, admit it and go look it up. As a fallible human being you will be more approachable than the omniscient giants we sometimes expect ourselves to be.

And "mistakes" can be remedied. If this discussion makes you feel that there are things you would like to have done differently, it is probably not too late. Attitudes, once instilled, can yet be changed. Elizabeth Canfield, prominent sex-education counselor, suggests: "It's a marvelous experience to walk up to a child and be able to say—'You know, I've done some more thinking about our discussion the other day and I've decided what I said didn't make sense (or it was a bunch of baloney, or garbage), so let's talk about it some more.' A child (or friend, neighbor, student, employee, lover) will be so delighted with this admission of your ability to blow it now and then, that a whole new world of communication will have opened up!"

One way for you to become more comfortable about talking about sex with children is to practice with adults. Share with your spouse or friends the questions you anticipate your child asking before they arise. Try out different ways of answering each question and then talk about which seem to fit best with your values and what you want for your child. You can take turns role-playing child and parent, giving each a turn to ask the questions a child might ask. After the "adult" in the pair responds to the "child's" questions, the "child" can report how it felt to be on the receiving end of the explanations offered, and the "adult" can share how it felt to be faced with these questions and to answer as he did. If first tries are not satisfactory, run the scene through again until you find an approach with which you are comfortable. Most people find that simply saying aloud words and phrases they had formerly only thought to themselves makes it easier to discuss sex.

Another deterrent to parents talking about sexuality with their children is the all-too-common belief that information equals permission. Not wanting to "put ideas in their heads," parents often behave as if the less their children know about sex, the better it will be for all concerned. This misguided protection is based on a false assumption. Children will have sexual feelings and interests whether or not adults acknowledge their children's sexuality. Sexual curiosity begins in the first months of life. Parents may be embarrassed or repressive about children's sexual behavior, but they cannot eliminate it without creating feelings which will handicap those children when they are grown up.

Information and knowledge do not cause damage, but secrecy and ignorance may. "No young girl was ever ruined by a book" is an old joke. But it is also true. Socially inappropriate behavior is more often the result of ignorance than of knowledge. None of us, child or adult, does everything we know to be possible. Nor do we want to. But when we know the score, we can choose which tune to sing, fitting the song to the scene and the characters with whom we share the platform.

Children need to know that they are not bad or unworthy because they are sexually curious about the bodies of others and have found sexual pleasure in their own bodies. But this does not mean that permission must extend for whatever they feel like doing with whomever they feel like doing it with. Parents can set limits on behavior without devaluing the child or his feelings. "I know you want to take your clothes off now, but when we're in the front yard I want you to wear your shorts," for example, establishes the parent's right to set limits without shaming the child or disparaging her feelings. If she then asks why, a parent may explain that there are times and places for being dressed or undressed and that front yards are one of the places where people have agreed that it is good manners to wear clothes.

Worrying about saying it just right sometimes stops parents from starting sexual discussions with children. Convinced that the right words are very important, they weigh each phrase, signaling to the children that the terrain is made of eggshells and can be approached only on tiptoes. Although their caution is exaggerated and probably defeats their intent of giving clear information, the words we choose do have an impact. Having the appropriate words enables children to understand the world, organize their thoughts, and behave in ways that make life with other people possible.

Adults often deliberately confuse children about sex. Because of their own discomfort, or convinced that the children "are too young to really understand," they use words that cloud rather than clarify the topic. Gadpaille mentions three ways that parents "contribute to childhood ignorance and confusion": by negative labeling, nonlabeling, and mislabeling.

We have already touched on negative labeling. Told that what he is doing is bad by a parent who sees his behavior as sexual, the child learns that he is bad, without being clear about what behavior is being criticized or what is wrong with it. How can he then not feel confused and anxious?

Not giving a child a vocabulary for sexuality is nonlabeling. Scolding or spanking a child who supposedly crosses the line of acceptable sexual behavior without telling her what she has done to warrant this, or distracting her from masturbating by offering another activity or physically interfering without comment, falls into this category. The result is that the child is left without the verbal building blocks to form positive sexual values.

"Finally," writes Gadpaille, "there is mislabeling. A child may be warned about supposedly harmful effects unrelated to the specifically sexual aspects of a particular behavior. For example, a masturbating girl may be told that she can hurt herself up inside. It is the sexual act that the adult wants to stop, but he mislabels it as physically dangerous, thus contributing to the child's misconception of sex as violent and harmful. Any false information, such as 'God put the seed in Mama's belly,' is mislabeling. Another form of mislabeling is the early identification of the sex organ by use of nursery or babytalk words which, in their initial application, refer to excretory functions. These words often are never replaced with sexually accurate words, and constitute a form of mislabeling that fosters the association between sexuality and dirtiness."

We don't need a lot of esoteric knowledge to avoid these pitfalls of language misuse. Rather than expertise, it requires a respect for the child's emotional and intellectual needs and the willingness to take responsibility for one's own feelings and demands. By saying "I know it feels good to touch your clitoris [or vulva], but it makes me uncomfortable when you do it in the kitchen, where I need to work; I would feel better if you would go to another room where you can have some privacy," a parent communicates his feelings and the limits he would like to place on the child's behavior without either mystifying or criticizing the child.

Although reproduction is more frequently and more easily discussed between parents and children than sexuality, many parents wonder when to tell their children about how people get babies. My opinion is that the child's own curiosity most often lets parents know when he wants information. When parents are reasonably comfortable responding to questions about sex and birth, and the environment is one in which babies are born to family, friends, or neighbors, children will ask for explanations of where and how these new additions came to be. Mother's pregnancy is, of course, the most interesting, promising the most upheaval in the child's own life. Even children whose circle of family and friends includes few births will begin to wonder about their own origins, asking where they were when Mommy and Daddy were in high school or visiting Mexico years before.

While the child's own curiosity should usually be a guide to the explicitness of your explanation, there are times when a parent should raise the topic without waiting to be asked. Too frequently parents wait for children to ask questions about sex while hoping that they won't. When a child shows no interest, fear of showing her feelings or lack of parental encouragement may underlie this supposed disinterest. Perhaps previous questions have been shrugged off by embarrassed parents who assumed that there would be plenty of time to deal with the subject when the child was older. Instead of taking advantage of an opportunity to casually provide simple, clear explanations, they may have inadvertently discouraged further questions.

When a child seems disinterested, parents can give him permission to express his questions by saying "When I was your age I used to have a lot of questions about sex—do you?" A loud "No" may mean that the child needs some time to get used to talking about a previously avoided subject, and should not be taken as the final word on the matter. Many opportunities occur in daily life to discuss sex and babies casually, without the pomp and ceremony of come-here-I-have-something-important-to-tell-you.

If a child notices that a school friend now has a new brother or sister, or a family pet has a litter, a parent may ask, "Do you know how people get babies?" If the child appears to want to know, this can be followed up with other questions until the child's level of understanding is clear, indicating where the parent needs to fill in missing pieces of the puzzle. Values as well as facts can be communicated in this way. The pregnancy of a teacher, aunt, or neighbor can provide an opportunity to discuss your feelings about having children by choice when parents are ready to take care of their young.

Once the subject has been raised, whether by you or by your child, the next important step is to find out what the child really wants to know. It is far better to tell your children what they want to know in terms they can understand than to inundate them with information. You will need to ask questions to find out what your child is *really* asking you. Lonnie Barbach tells of one three-and-a-half-year-old who "asked Diane, 'How does a car work?' Diane's mind immediately raced to all the complexities of a combustion engine. . . . But before she jumped in over both their heads, Diane asked, 'How do you think it works?' 'Well, I don't think you push it with your feet,' the child answered. This greatly simplified Diane's problem as she explained the absolute rudiments of a motor attached to the wheels which causes the car to move."

There's an old joke that makes the same point: Five-year-old Johnny comes home and asks his mother, "Where did I come from?" His flustered but well-meaning mother launches into a long explanation of reproduction, including sexual intercourse and conception. Impatiently, Johnny interrupts her, protesting, "I know all that. But Jimmy says he comes from Detroit. Where do I come from?"

Responding to the child who asks, "Where do babies come from?" with "What do you think?" lets you know what the child knows or guesses. Questions like these reveal misinformation or troublesome fantasies the child may be having. They prepare the ground for parents' answers, which may then be geared to the child's level of comprehension.

Never make children feel stupid or foolish because they look at reproduction in a fanciful way. Don't be afraid to let them know that you enjoy the inventiveness of their imagery. You can support children's problem-solving effort without confirming their erroneous impressions. For example, to a child who answers "the mommy swallows a seed" to the question of how babies get started, a parent might respond: "I can see why you might think that. Most things that go in our bodies go first through our mouths, when we eat." She would then go on to explain that the baby grows in a special place called the uterus, not in the stomach, and that this special place has entrances and exits separate from those to and from the stomach. Sometimes children's words may seem like nonsense to an adult, but they do have meaning for the child. Listening with respect to what they have to say, putting their remarks in the context of what is happening in their lives—immediate events or timely themes— reveals the underlying meaning of their comments.

You will probably be surprised by some of what your children tell you. In Chapters 3 through 8, we will look in detail at what children at different levels of comprehension *do* think about how people get babies. Most of the parents of the children I interviewed could not predict their offspring's responses to my questions, consistently overestimating their children's level of understanding. One mother who read an article I had published in *Psychology Today* later told me: "I said to myself, 'Oh, my kids wouldn't think anything that silly.'" So she went home and asked her nine-

and eleven-year-olds what they were thinking, and was surprised to hear that the nine-year-old said he was guessing and the eleven-year-old had not long ago abandoned a theory involving a long line of blue and pink bassinets. "And I thought these kids had been told all this stuff," she reported to me. "It really made me realize that children don't quite get things the way you thought they would when you told them. It was really amazing to me." She was also pleased to find that her fifth-grader, who had previously avoided all talk of sex, followed up on her opening the subject by bringing her questions he had about films in the school's sex-education program.

Learning what children are thinking helps adults make sure the foundation for understanding is sound before going on to build elaborate explanations. But it is not enough to answer their questions with questions. The child who is asked only "Well, what do you think about that?" and is given no further information will get the message that parents are not willing to share their own knowledge and feelings. Before long, he will stop bringing his questions to those who evade answering.

While there is no way of avoiding all misunderstanding, some ways of presenting information are less confusing than others. It is so much better to have a dialogue with your child than to lecture without checking out what he or she is doing with the information you provide. The dialogue might begin, "Well, how do you think it happens?" A parent would then validate the child's problem-solving effort, confirm what was accurate in the child's account, clear up or sort out confusing threads, and then find out what it is the child wants to know more about. Children often know their own limits, deciding to forgo some information until they have processed what they already know. One woman, responding to her daughter's expressed uneasiness about birth, asked her, "Would you like me to tell you more about what it's like?" And the girl said, "No." "I have all I can deal with at the moment" came across without being said.

Do not be discouraged if your child comes to you with a question you thought you had answered long ago. Being told something once is not enough for a child to learn, whether it is about sex or geography or friendship. Children seem to need repetition to firmly implant new concepts in their previous understanding of the world. As they work toward ever more complex integrations of the same subject matter, from time to time they may feel confused.

Maturation is not a steady progression of acquiring stable and permanent abilities. "Two steps forward and one step back" probably best describes how it feels to make gains, backslide, and gain again, perhaps more easily the next time. This regression to earlier ways of behaving or thinking about the world is a normal part of development. As development proceeds, children will reevaluate and discard former misconceptions, organizing past learning to include present experience. To do this successfully, they need parents to give them emotional support, the security that permits exploration. It is easier to venture forth into unknown territories when we know that we can touch home base when we need to.

3

The Geographers—
Level One

Level One children believe that babies have always existed. These children range in age from three to seven. They
are likely to answer the question How do people get babies?
as if it were a question about geography. Their only problem is accounting for the whereabouts of babies before they
arrive at the family hearth. They typically choose three locations for the storage of babies prior to birth. Based on their
own experience getting new things, they may assume babies
are bought in stores. Or perhaps the purchase takes place at
the hospital. If they have been told that God arranges the
arrival of babies, they may picture "God's place" as a
heavenly hacienda or cloud-soft nursery. Most often, though,
because of their own observations or what they have been told
by parents, they think of the baby as in the mother's body
before birth. Several parents have told me about their toddlers looking under mama's skirt to see the baby, untucking
her blouse in further search when earlier explorations did
not reveal the baby they had been told was there.

These children also believe that all children become grown-
ups and all grown-ups are mommies and daddies. As babies
begin to grow automatically, as part of the maturational
process, so all girls grow to be mommies and all boys become daddies. They may even be mommies and daddies
without having children. But if they do not as yet have children, that is just a matter of time. If they eat their vegetables

and want babies enough, they will have them. And to not want babies is, to these young children, unthinkable. Nurturing babies and little children is an important and as valuable as any human activity. It means ministering to *them*.

Whether informed or misinformed by parents and friends, children's thinking about how people get babies will depend on their problem-solving ability. How they think will mold what they think. They will listen to others' accounts, adopting some, discarding some, in their efforts to reconstruct their own version of creation.

As adults, we often take for granted concepts that children can only learn gradually. In thinking about the origin of babies, children begin to grapple with two concepts integral to the unraveling of life's mysteries: identity and causality.

Identity

However much my appearance may have changed as I grew and matured, my identity is constant and my sense of self is conserved despite the transformations I may see in my mirror over the years. It is only when I recognize that you and I are the same people we have always been that I can think about my own origins and those of my brothers and sisters.

Jimmy is three years old. After our interview his mother handed him some of his baby pictures for him to show me. He looked at a picture of himself taken two years earlier and said, "That's Mikey." Mikey, his younger brother, closely resembled the infant in the picture. Anyone might have made the same mistake. His mother corrected him: "I know it looks like Mikey, but that was you when you were a baby." And Jimmy asked, "That was me when I was Mikey?"

Sparky is a young brown-and-white pony. He lives in the yard of a nursery school. One day Marsha, the nursery-school teacher, brought in a picture of herself as a four-year-old seated on a brown-and-white pony. And all of the children asked, "Is that Sparky you're riding?"

For these youngsters, appearance is all-important in determining identity. We can imagine that children's thinking goes something like this: If I used to look just like my brother perhaps I used to be my brother. If the brown-and-white pony I ride at age four looks just like the pony my teacher rode when she was four, it must be the same pony.

Young children asked to identify each member of a large family in a series of photographs begin by denying the identity of anyone who does not look exactly alike in both pictures. If a child has changed dresses or cut her hair, they will reject the possibility that she is the same person. They cannot discriminate between the essential and the inessential aspects of who's who. A little later they will base their identifications on more ephemeral things: "He's the same boy because he's got straight hair" or "because he's got sunglasses," "She's the same girl because she has a pretty dress" or "because she's got curly hair." (Lemke.) Identities can be handed down with used clothing.

It is not until they are six or seven that children let go of the belief that magical transformations are possible. In a study by Lawrence Kohlberg, most four-year-olds said that a girl could be a boy if she wanted to, or if she played boy games, or if she wore a boy's hair style or clothes. They also claimed that a cat could be a dog if it wanted to, or if its whiskers were cut off. By six or seven, most children were insistent that neither cat nor girl could change species or sex regardless of changes in appearance or behavior. They had learned that identity is permament and cannot be disrupted by apparent transformations.

Causality

As children learn to conserve identity, they are also developing the concept of causality. It is only when children begin to perceive that events and phenomena have causes that they can attempt to investigate what those causes are. It is not immediately obvious that today's events may be related to yesterday's deeds that made them happen. To be able to accurately link two activities in a "because" statement, children must first explore the relationships that are most noticeable and pertinent to them.

The same child who tells you that one boat floats "because it's red" may tell you that another floats "because it's blue" or "because it's big." Size and color are the boat's most outstanding features. Therefore, the child feels that floating must be explainable by these very apparent dominant characteristics.

A little later, children are less random in their explanations. Instead, the world becomes a utopia organized by the people for the people. Children explain origins in psychological or moral language. Night falls so that we may go to sleep, and trees grow so that we may eat fruit. I cannot watch Ellen's dreams because she doesn't want me to see them. Cows moo because they don't want to talk people talk. And children have the mommies and daddies they do because those were the parents they wanted.

As we explore the different levels of children's thinking about the origin of babies, we will see how their concept of causality develops from these primitive beginnings to an understanding in harmony with the Western scientific thought that dominates our culture.

Level One. Geography

The youngest children answered the question, "How do people get babies?" as if it were a question about geography. These children, usually three to five years old, told me:

"You go to a baby store and buy one."
"You get babies from tummies."
"Babies come from God's place."
"It just grows inside Mommy's tummy. It's there all the time. Mommy doesn't have to do anything. She just waits until she feels it."

These children assume that babies, like themselves and all those who people their world, have always existed. The problem is only to discover where the baby was before it came to live wherever it is now.

A 1975 "Dennis the Menace" cartoon captures the essence of the child's assumption that he has always existed. The illustration shows Dennis and his parents in a darkened room, watching a home movie. On the screen, his parents, dressed in tuxedo and wedding gown, are being showered with rice by smiling people as a minister waves good-bye. The caption has Dennis complaining, "I s'pose I was home with the sitter while all this was goin' on."

How can the world have existed before he did? How can his parents, in whose lives he is so prominent, have lived without him? Toys exist because he plays with them. His dog Ruff is there because Dennis loves him. Mother makes it night by turning out the light so that he can go to sleep. A world so clearly organized around him could not have preceded him. The egocentrism of the young child leads him inevitably to the conclusion that he must have always existed. A world without him is inconceivable.

But all these other babies. They weren't always here. Each child remembers a time when some younger child was not around. Where did she come from? Where did they get him? Children hear stories about their own birth, about the time before they were in their family, and can only conclude that they must have been some place else. Where then?

Children typically think of one of three places in trying to account for where babies were warehoused before birth.

NINE POUNDS FOUR OUNCES AT $1.50 A POUND

"Mommy bought me in a shop," a four-year-old boy told Piaget fifty years ago. Several of the children I talked with recently made the same claim. Since almost everything new that comes into their lives is bought, new babies must also come from a store.

Nina told me: "Babies come from their houses. You can buy some babies in somebody's house." She is four.

Dick, nearly four, would give this advice to people who wanted to be parents: "First you has to go, go to a baby store and buy a baby." I asked him, "Have you ever seen a baby store?"

DICK: No.

ME: Do you think there are some?

DICK: Yeah. Yeah, way far away. Right up there. From the hill.

ME: And people go there?

DICK: Yeah. I went there yesterday, and I saw babies. I heard them cry but I didn't even look at them. I just heard them cry. So I think you buy one if it cries, if you don't want him to cry you just have to put his head on his stomach and that means he doesn't cry any more. Yeah, that's how you buy a baby.

Grant, just three, claims to have seen such a store. I asked him how people get babies. "Buy them," he said, "from the baby store." Had he seen such a store? "Yeah." But were there babies there? "Yeah, our sister. She was sleeping on a shelf."

Grant, like Dick, was redecorating his memory to match his experience that new acquisitions come from commercial transactions. But, with an egalitarian flair, Grant sees children as consumers as well as goods in the family marketplace.

ME: How come Laurie's your mommy?

GRANT: Cause that's my mom, and dad.

ME: How come?

GRANT: 'Cause I wanted them. Tara [his sister] and me buyed them. I buyed a daddy and Tara buyed a mommy.

This turnabout, asserting that it is children who choose their parents rather than parents who arrange to have children, denies the very real imbalance of power between adults and their preschool children and illustrates the weight children give to their own wishes.

The Heavenly Nursery

Another popular location for storing babies prior to their arrival at the family hearth is "God's place." Few of the children I talked with believed that babies were "bundles from heaven." Instead, they located unborn infants in their mother's bodies or in the marketplace. I imagine, however, that in communities where religion plays a more influential role in people's lives, parents' teaching that babies are a gift from God would satisfy the curiosity of the preschooler, who requires only a geographical location to account for the origin of babies.

Many adults have told me that their early childhood beliefs resembled greeting-card cartoons of birth: hundreds of babies lolling around on clouds, passing the time in friendly play until it comes time to be taken, by stork or heavenly messenger, to their waiting parents.

MOMMY'S BODY

Alexandra will soon be four. She told me that a baby "just grows inside Mommy's tummy. It's there all the time. Mommy doesn't have to do anything. She just waits until she feels it." We continued to talk:

ME: How did your brother start to be in your mommy's tummy?

ALEXANDRA: Um, my baby just went in my mommy's tummy.

ME: How did he go in?

ALEXANDRA: He was just in my mommy's tummy.

ME: Before you said that he wasn't there when you were there. Was he?

ALEXANDRA: Yeah, and then he was in the other place . . . in America.

ME: In America?

ALEXANDRA: Yeah, in somebody else's tummy. And then he went through somebody's vagina, and then he went in my mommy's tummy.

ME: In whose tummy was he before?

ALEXANDRA: I don't know who his—her name is. It's a her.

For this little girl, typical of the Level One children, a baby that now exists must always have existed. The only real question is where he was before he came to live at her house. She knows that her brother grew inside her mother's body. The question of how and when he started to grow there are beyond her grasp at the moment, but she extrapolates from the information she has: Babies grow inside tummies and come out vaginas. If there was a time prior to her brother's being in her mother's tummy, then he must have been in some place else, in somebody else's tummy, and that somebody else must be female, because "only big girls can grow babies in their tummies." Presumably this chain can go on indefinitely, with each mommy getting her baby in turn from another woman.

Penny, too, sees a baby as a gift that is passed around until it is finally given to its mother. I asked her, "How do people get babies?"

PENNY: My mommy does. She gets babies.

ME: How?

PENNY: She gets her baby from Bill [Penny's father]. From Peggy.

ME: How does Peggy get the baby?

PENNY: She got it from Peter [who gets it] from Danny [who gets it] from me.

ME: How did you get the baby?

PENNY: From my dad.

ME: From your dad? How did that happen?

PENNY: I got it from my 'nother, my big sister. Well, my sister's name is Lisa. Well, next Mommy got from Lisa.

Most of the children saw no need to string together a series of locations for the baby before birth. If the baby grows inside its mommy's body, then it must always have been there. Alexandra was dislodged from her initial belief that babies were always in mommies' tummies by being called to account for her brother's whereabouts when she was in their mother's tummy. Jacob felt no need to resort to geographical guesses about his sister. Quite willing to share the occupancy of their mother's body, he told me joyfully: "Tina and I were in the womb together. We were hugging in the womb."

Most of these children were either unenlightened or had forgotten that there was a special place for babies to grow inside Mommy. They told me the baby grows in Mommy's tummy or stomach. A few, however, described babies as coming from Mommy's breasts. Three-year-old Sandra told me people get babies "out of geegees [breasts]."

SANDRA: Like this, they come out [waving her arm away from her chest]. They've got to get milk in the geegees then. Babies come out of geegees.

ME: Whose geegees do they come out from?

SANDRA: Everybody's.

ME: Do they come out of yours?

SANDRA: When I grow up.

For the children of nursing mothers, babies and breasts are as strongly linked as peanut butter and jelly. Since only women have developed breasts and only women grow babies, breasts must figure prominently in the origins of babies. An anthropological parallel is found among the Sinaupolo aborigines, who believe conception takes place in the breasts since these first show signs of the women's condition.

I continued to question Sandra:

ME: Do babies come out of daddies' geegees?

SANDRA: Noooooo.

ME: Mommies'?

SANDRA: Yes.

ME: Why don't they come out of daddies?

SANDRA: Because their body has hair.

A few children thought that girl babies come from mommies and boy babies come from daddies, presumably based on the principle that "like begets like," with each parent reproducing his or her own kind of person. But this response was uncommon. When asked if babies grow in daddies' tummies, and if not, why not, most children at this level stated "they just don't" without being able to explain why. Others, like Sandra, focus on an easily observable sex difference that bears no obvious connection to childbearing. Three-year-old Penny based her conclusion on daddies' inability to feed the baby "because daddies got little nipples and mommies got big nipples." Jeff, who is four, told me: "Babies come out of mommies' tummies. They just crawl through the tunnel. Daddies just don't have tunnels like mommies do," so, of course, babies cannot grow in their tummies. His success in making a causal link builds on his accurate grasp of anatomy.

The characteristic limitation of all children at this first level, however accurate their understanding of basic anatomy, is their inability to account in any way for the baby's beginning to grow in its mother's body. Penny's response is typical: "They just grow inside. I don't know how it starts. It just grows." When queried further, they fall back on one of two sets of assumptions: Babies are in girls' tummies all the time and begin to develop as the girls mature into women, or wishing or choosing to be a mother starts the baby off.

Jeff's account of birth is based on the assumption that babies occur spontaneously. I asked him how he would explain about where babies came from to someone who didn't know anything about it.

JEFF: I'd tell them that how you get a baby is: They come out of your tummy.

ME: What if they said, "Well, that sounds like a good idea, but I don't think there's a baby in my tummy. How do I get a baby to be in my tummy?"

JEFF: Just live.

ME: What if they live a long, long time and no baby has started to grow. Do they have to do something to make it grow?

JEFF: Just wait a long time. Just wait.

Spontaneous birth has as a companion concept universal parenthood. Childbearing is seen as part of the inexorable process of growing up, and all grown-ups are ipso facto parents. Categories or definitions of mommies and daddies are not yet developed. Later children will know that it is the begetting and taking care of children that make a parent. Now "a mommy is a grown-up lady," and "all ladies are mommies." To become a daddy a boy need only "eat vegetables" and "get taller and taller." And if they have no children? No matter. They're still mommies and daddies.

ME: How do mommies get to be mommies?

JEFF: I guess they just grow like mommies.

ME: They grow like mommies, and then they're grown-up women.

JEFF: Right.

ME: Are all grown-up women mommies?

JEFF: Yes.

ME: What if they don't have any children? Are they still mommies?

JEFF: They're just mommies anyway.

ME: What is a mommy?

JEFF: A mommy could talk, a mommy could get angry, a mommy could get happy.

ME: What is a daddy?

JEFF: He does work, and he could talk, and he's alive. He could get mad, like mommies could, but my dad is bigger than my mommy.

Asked to define a mommy or a daddy, these children describe activities or characteristics of their own parents. They cannot yet separate the essential from the coincidental ("a mommy paints"), nor can they abstract from the collection of daddies they know to form a category.

Jenny told me: "I have a baby for you. It's in my stomach. It's coming out Thurs—in five days." It's hard to say how deeply held this belief is. The time of exit, at least, seems fanciful. Tina, hitting her belly during acrobatics, cried out, "Oh, that hurts my baby in my tummy!" Rita, at four and a half, described how there are little babies in little girls.

ME: How do daddies get to be daddies?

TITA: Oh, when the boys . . . the boys are a baby, and then
they grow up to a man. The boys grow up to be a man.
And they're grown-ups.

ME: But how do they get to be daddies? There are grown-
ups who aren't daddies, aren't there?

RITA: Grown-ups are daddies or mommies.

ME: What if a grown-up doesn't have any children?

RITA: That's okay. Then the babies are still in the stomach,
and then the babies grow to little girls and big girls.

ME: So, if somebody doesn't have any children yet, what
does that mean?

RITA: That means the babies are in the stomach. I already
have a baby in my stomach.

ME: You have a baby growing in your stomach now?

RITA: No, it won't grow 'cause I'm little. When I'm big, then
it can grow. You might loose the baby. You have to
be very, very careful because the baby may get loose
in your stomach.

Like Jenny, Tina, and many other little girls, Rita identi-
fied with her mother during her recent pregnancy. She
liked to play that she too was about to give birth, walking
funny, holding her back as she sat down, making plans for
her new baby. The line between play fantasy and reality was
not always clear. But her belief in the baby in her own
stomach is also based on an intuitive deduction. Like so
many children her age who believe that babies "just grow"
and that an adult woman who is not yet a mother already
has within her the baby she will inevitably parent, Rita sees
little girls as having even littler babies within them. Picture
nested hollow wooden dolls: As you open each doll you
find a smaller but identical version of the same painted face
and costume; only the artist's limits in working with small
objects prevent the series from being infinite. This toy ap-
peals to children. It makes their view of the continuity of
generations concrete.

Little boys, too, may think that babies have been inside
mommies since long ago. "I started to be in my mommy's

tummy when she grew up real tall," said Alan, almost five. "They're just there all the time," three-year-old Mitchell told me.

ME: Does your mommy have a baby in her tummy now?

MITCHELL: No.

ME: How come?

MITCHELL: Because I saw the baby when he walked upstairs.

ME: What baby?

MITCHELL: Jacob.

ME: Could she have another baby in her tummy?

MITCHELL: No.

ME: How come?

MITCHELL: Because she just doesn't. She won't have another baby. Because two, because one baby is just enough.

For Mitchell, *baby* is not an abstract category including all those children recently or soon to be born. It refers only to the concrete existence of the only baby in his life, his little brother. Tina, not quite three, thinks of her mother's unborn child as Angeline, the only baby she now knows. In their conceptual worlds, identity is not yet fixed, constant, and irreversible. Angeline may be all babies, and Jacob the only baby.

It is not only babies whose identities are arbitrary or transient. Children's own identities and those of their parents are similarly in flux. Penny told me, "I can have my mommy be inside me. My mommy's got a tummy. I grow up and be her, be her mommy, and she grows inside my tummy." Erica, also three, announced to her mother that she and her brother were going to grow up and "be you": "Danny will be the daddy and I will be the mommy, and you and Daddy will be Grandma and Grandpa." In listening to her, her mother had the clear sense that she was not just talking about adopting different social roles, but of their all becoming other people. The mechanics of these transformations were explained to me by another three-year-old friend, who told me that she would be my mommy when she "grew up" and I "grew down."

Wishes are not just the stuff from which dreams are made for young children. The heady power of an assumed thought-magic leads them to believe that wishing something makes it happen. Despite their very real powerlessness, they tend to see the world as organized around their desires and behavior. To be realistic about their own helplessness would pose a crushing handicap to their developing assertiveness and competence. Their egocentrism is not without dangers, however, for the actual turn of events can be frustrating. If a sister dies, if parents divorce, if a teacher gets sick, children often assume that their own anger or misdeeds are responsible for these calamities.

There is a happier side to the magical omnipotence of young children. When asked to explain how come they have the mommies and daddies they do, they regularly claim to have chosen their parents: "Because I like this mommy" or "because I wanted to have a daddy and he gets me." Some even insist that if they didn't like this daddy or this mommy, they would "get a different one." "If I didn't love him," said Lisa, "I'd have a different Dad." Luckily, this assumption remains unchallenged. All the children I talked with like and plan to keep the parents they have.

If they think themselves powerful, they know their parents to be even more so. Young children often assume that whatever their parents want to do they do, and whatever they do they want to do. Alan's mommy is his mommy " 'cause she wanted to be my mommy," and daddies get to be daddies by wanting to be. Seth's sister started to grow in his mommy's tummy because "my mama wanted her to be in there." Some of this recognition of parental power may come from what they have been told by parents who emphasize choice in family planning. But for the children, the desire and the decision are sufficient to make the plan a reality.

A mommy is a mommy is a mommy. But by any other name, she would be somebody else. It is difficult for young children to comprehend that their teacher may *also* be a mommy or that their mommy may *also* be a doctor. What is most important, so important that it overshadows all the other roles she may play, is her relationship to *them*. Mommies get to be mommies, said Alan, because "they just decided to have that name." Grown-up ladies start to be mommies, according to Sally, "when people call them mommies." And Jim is Leslie's daddy " 'cause I wanted to call him 'Daddy.' " By giving somebody else a name or renaming oneself, old identities may be discarded and new ones adopted. It is only through diligent repetition and some maturation that children learn that "names will never harm them." For a long time, names are very powerful, and you are what you are called.

Talking with Pre–Level One Children

So, now that you know how a child at Level One is likely to think, what can you do with this information? In the "Talking with Children" sections in Chapters 3 through 8, I will discuss how to use what you have learned about children's thinking about sex and birth at each of the six levels. In general, it is a good idea to talk with a child in language which represents one level above where he now is. In this chapter, we will begin with issues to consider in talking with children not yet firmly at Level One.

When your Level One or pre-Level One child asks, "Where do babies come from?" that is just what he wants to know: where? In what place was this baby before it came here? In answering their questions and introducing the subject of new babies, it is best to begin with the geography of reproduction.

Even very young children can begin to understand that a new baby is growing in Mommy's body, although they will need to be told more than once. Children not quite three have told me that the baby is in Mommy's womb and will come out through her vagina. Still younger, preverbal children will lift Mommy's skirt or smock, expecting to see the baby they have been told is in her belly.

A study done more than a generation ago concluded that it is not until they are nine or ten that children first begin to notice and discuss the mother's distended abdomen during pregnancy. I found that even children of two and three had these observations.

Think of how short preschoolers are and how much time they spend looking up at their mothers. What is remarkable and requires explanation is not that they can and do observe the change in her profile during pregnancy, but that this observation is not universal. To not notice such a dramatic change requires a good reason. Most psychologists have traditionally explained children's failure to notice pregnancy as selective inattention to unwanted information. Because they are jealous of their mother's affection, not wanting to share her with a new arrival, they refuse to recognize what they do not want to admit.

While this kind of denial doubtless occurs, it is not the only or even the most prevalent reason why children fail to recognize the fact of pregnancy. More often they lack the labels and conceptual tools to draw conclusions from their observations. If you cannot add, two and two do not equal four, but only two and another two. Mommy's belly may be no larger than those of Grandma and Uncle Joe, who are overweight, not pregnant. Even when Mommy brings the baby home from the hospital, her untutored toddler has no reason to connect his new sister with Mommy's former girth. He has not yet learned to spin the thread of cause and effect between the two events.

When she was three years old, my friend Ana challenged her nursery-school teacher, Jamie. Jamie had just told the children gathered around her, listening to her account of birth, that babies grow inside their mommies' tummies. "No they don't," countered Ana. Jamie patiently explained again. Ana was pleasant but firm. Finally, three repetitions later,

Jamie asked Ana where *she* thought the baby was before birth. "In the mommy's uterus," she answered.

Ana was defending a vital distinction. It is important to teach children that the baby has a special growing place within the mother's body. Children need to know that this special growing place, called the *womb* or *uterus,* is different from and unconnected to the tummy or stomach. Most of the time, some confusion about the precise location of the baby has no ill effects. Occasionally, however, confusion can generate concern.

Jeanne was happy and excited. A new baby was going to come and live at her house, she told her nursery-school teachers. At school, she would pretend to be pregnant, walking with her belly out and her hands at the small of her back. Then one day, with no warning and no word of explanation, she stopped eating. She refused all food both at home and at school. On the fifth day of her enigmatic fast, her worried mother came to school to talk with her teachers about what was going on.

One of her teachers, Rosemary, sat down with Jeanne in the fantasy corner of the schoolroom. They played and told each other stories, and Rosemary learned why Jeanne refused to eat. In her fantasy, Jeanne had a baby in her tummy, just like Mommy. Were she to eat, all that yukky food would bury her wonderful baby. Rather than dump garbage on the fantasied fetus, she denied herself all nourishment. Rosemary explained to her that the place where the baby was had no passageway to either mouth or stomach, but opened only to the vagina, its only entrance and exit. Jeanne, reassured, accepted food from that time on.

Not all children draw the same conclusions Jeanne did. And, of those who do conjure up the same images, most do not attach the same destructive meaning. Alan, for example, told me how he received nourishment before birth.

ALAN: When my mommy ate food, it came to me. Yeah, and it was already crunched up in pieces, so I could eat it.

ME: Is that when you were still inside her?

ALAN: Yeah.

ME: How did you eat it?

ALAN: Well, I didn't eat the food. I didn't eat the things that you would eat with your teeth. Just swallowed the things that you drink. I couldn't chew.

Alan, like Jeanne, had a picture of the food the mother chews falling down to the baby within her. Unlike Jeanne, he saw this as an ingenious way to feed the growing baby. His tone was one of happy discovery. One important difference lies in his not having fantasies of pregnancy, although many small boys do play at being pregnant. Preschool boys may tell their friends that they want to be mommies when they grow up. They do not yet understand that gender identity is forever.

There is a more general lesson to be learned from the different responses Alan and Jeanne had to their shared misapprehension. It is not the confusion itself but the *meaning* each child assigns his or her vision of events that determines its emotional consequences. A dog may be a beloved playmate or a dangerous beast. Growing up may be eagerly anticipated as promising competence and freedom or fearfully resisted as bringing only heavy responsibility and deterioration. Another author wrote about a little girl who placed books on her head to stunt her growth. If she did not grow up, she reasoned, she would not die. Her actions and her feelings, like Jeanne's, can be understood only by exploring the private emotional meanings evoked by her intellectual conclusions.

Childish beliefs that babies grow in stomachs seldom lead to such dramatic consequences as Jeanne's fasting. They can produce anxiety about eating, especially when children learn that babies grow from "seeds," so abundant in fruit. Having a bowel movement, whereby one might unwittingly and uncontrollably lose a baby thought to be in the stomach, can also be worrisome to the confused child.

Many parents do not even attempt to teach children that

the baby grows in the uterus, not the stomach. For one thing, it's a hard word for many children to pronounce. For another, the tummy may be seen as everything located between the breasts and the genitals. If a mother points to her own body and explains, "The baby grows down here, not up there in the stomach," her child may reply, "Well, that's your tummy too."

Parents would do well not to let the matter drop there. As we have seen, this is an important distinction, which may require more explanation. The parent can continue:

PARENT: That's what most people call the "tummy." And when a woman is pregnant, it looks like the tummy is growing big. But the uterus [or womb] is in there, pretty close to the tummy, and that's the thing that's really growing.

The child may have some questions at this point. Further clarification may be needed before continuing.

PARENT: Then, when the baby is ready to be born, it is pushed out of the uterus through a tunnel in the mommy. That tunnel is called the "vagina," and nothing can get in or out of the uterus except through the vagina. It's the only tunnel to the uterus. The mouth has a tunnel to the stomach, but it doesn't have a tunnel to the uterus. The vagina goes from the uterus on one end to the vulva on the other end. And that's where the baby comes out.

It is important to add that the vagina is neither the urethral nor the anal opening, but a passageway in women to the special growing place for babies.

Some of the language I have been using may seem like big words for small children. I believe children need to know and have the right to be told the names for body parts and processes. Their tongues may stumble over some of the trickier sounds, so that "bagina" or "gina" may substitute for "vagina" for a while, but this is preferable to the "cuteness" of pet names that may hinder communication between children from different families. Even when they choose to use slang, children gain confidence from knowing the "real" words.

Children need to know the anatomical differences between boys and girls. Some of this learning takes place through explorations they conduct on their own, with brothers and sisters, playmates, and in the nursery-school bathroom. It is important that parents supplement their children's "self-help" efforts at sexual enlightenment, giving them names for parts of their own bodies and those of the other sex. Direct instructions by parents about female anatomy is especially useful, since the female sexual parts are more hidden and less handled than testicles and penis. If both sexes know about vulva, clitoris, vagina, and uterus, boys and girls are less likely to see each other as sexual "haves" and "have-nots."

Psychoanalytic theory tells us that both boys and girls attach superior value to having a penis and think of girls as having been damaged because they lack this wonderful organ. Little girls then conclude that little boys are naturally superior. Boys agree, and, having seen that girls have "nothing" where their penises should be, fear that they too will be punished by losing their sex organs. One sometimes gets the impression, in reading Freud, that femininity is a deficiency disease for which there is no cure.

There is considerable potential for increasing self-esteem in girls and reducing devaluation of girls by boys in teaching both about female sexual anatomy. The four-year-old boys who told me that babies don't grow in daddies because "daddies don't have uteruses [or "tunnels"]" don't think of girls as damaged boys but as having different structures for a good reason. Little girls, lacking the breasts which are the most obvious signs of their mothers' sexual identity, can find reassurance in knowing that they already have a uterus and a vagina for having babies and a clitoris and a vagina for sexual pleasure.

Talking about where babies are before birth provides an excellent opportunity to teach about sexual differences, although this information can be introduced on other occasions as well. A child's "Where do babies come from?" is an obvious time to begin to talk about sex and birth. Helping to diaper a baby or bathing with a sister, brother, or playmate may be other times when a child is inclined to talk about sex differences and reproduction.

Often children don't ask about the origin of babies before they need to know. When do they need to know? Either when all the other kids know or when parents are expecting a new baby, whichever comes first. Children may feel ashamed of their ignorance when talked down to by knowing play-mates. More important, they need information which will help them out as they anticipate the changes in their lives that will occur after a sister or brother is born. Will their parents still love them? Will Mother still have time for them? Will Father still pay attention to them, take them for walks, tell them stories? Where has Mommy gone when she's away for several days? Will she ever come back? Children fear they will be displaced in their parents' affection.

"My mommy doesn't want no babies. She always wants to take care of me, to have me," Daria told me. Why does Mommy want a new baby when she already has me? They wonder and worry about the intruder who will disrupt the world as they know it. Where did he come from? Why is she here? How will life be different?

Judy was three years old when her sister was born. Immediately after the birth, she made the rounds of the rela-tives. Starting with her mother, she asked, "Are you still my mommy?" She asked each family member in turn: "Are you still my daddy?" "Are you still my auntie?" etc. Like all children, Judy thought of the new baby as replacing the old one. She needed to be reassured that her mother can be both the baby's mommy and her mommy too, that Daddy has love and care enough for two children, and that she is still a valued member of the family and not a displaced person.

Children need to be able to share their concerns about

pregnancy. They need reassurance that their fears will not become reality. We have already seen that they may fear that the baby who inherits their crib will also take possession of all parental affection. They may also worry about Mommy's health and welfare.

Jeff, who was not quite four, was eating lunch with his pregnant mother. "Oh, Mommy, my tummy's very full and your tummy's *very* full!" he exclaimed. His mother explained that her tummy would get bigger and bigger as the baby grew. Jeff was concerned: "Oh, Mommy, your tummy will break." He feared she would burst, like a balloon blown too large. He needed to know that her skin and muscles could stretch as big as the baby.

Later, his mother pointed out the baby's movement to him: "Feel the baby kicking." Jeff, trained to be a peaceable child, didn't think that was right. "It's bad to kick. The baby shouldn't do that." A muscle pain registered on his mother's face, and Jeff demanded, "Did that baby hurt you?" A baby who kicks is violent and hurtful. A less-aggressive word, such as "squirming" or "moving," evokes less painful images.

Even toddlers can be prepared for the arrival of a new baby in the family. Children understand language even before they can use it to express their own thoughts. The younger the child, the less she will understand, but some base will have been laid for the important events to follow. There are several picture books on the market which show families with small children preparing for a birth. Even children too young to speak can look at these pictures, hear the text read to them, and begin to sense that something like that might well happen in their house.

Children love to hear stories about their own beginnings. Hearing about what Mommy and Daddy did to prepare for *their* birth, where they went and how they planned, helps children feel part of the welcoming team for the new baby. It is easier for them to accept the love and nurturance devoted to the new baby when they themselves feel loved and assured that they received the same care and generated the same excitement. Stories that begin "When you were a baby you used to . . . and I used to . . ." and go on to share a pleasant memory will always find a receptive audience.

When children in his nursery school played "London Bridge," Eddie excitedly announced that he had been in London "when I was in my mommy's womb." London was, therefore, a very special place to him. Lilah told me with pride, "My mom didn't feed me baby food, she fed me only fresh stuff, and I ate it all up, because I loved it." Knowing about themselves as babies, seeing how much they have changed, gives them a sense of their history and continuing identity.

As a guideline for when and how much to tell children, one therapist lists five things children should know by the time they are three or four:

1. They should know the names of the body's sexual parts.

2. They should know the socially shared words for elimination.

3. They should understand the basic fact that babies grow within the mother's body.

4. They should know enough anatomy by direct observation to understand the differences between boys and girls, even of they can't explain how they know.

5. If they want to know and ask about it, they should also know that babies are made by mothers and fathers together.

All this information is within the grasp of the preschool child.

4

The Manufacturers—
Level Two

When a child reaches Level Two, usually between four and eight, he recognizes that an explanation is required by the question How do people get babies? A location where they can be found is not enough to account for the process, and they know it. In trying to figure out the origin of babies, however, they are limited to their own experience of body parts and what each part does, and they also take into consideration the ways they have seen other objects created. A Level Two child knows that babies have not always existed, they must be manufactured. In this way, babies are not unlike other natural phenomena, like mountains, rivers, and storms. For these children, everything in the world has been constructed either by people or by God with magical powers.

Alternatively, children may think that parents are limited to the bodily experiences that children have themselves known. The "digestive fallacy"—the belief that babies get into a woman's body by being swallowed and get out when she moves her bowels—is a generalization from their own body processes. Still egocentric, they assume their own experience is a yardstick of what's possible in the world.

A few of the children at this level assign Father a role in the birth drama, but most of these fit what they have been told to a mechanical process. Father may plant his

seed by hand or use his penis to push the seed into its fur-
row. Magical thinking often broad-jumps critical but elusive
steps. Perhaps parents need only lie in the same bed together;
the sperm may leap from one to the other with no contact
necessary, or maybe it rolls across the sheets from father to
mother. The physical processes that adults know from personal experience are as fantastic and farfetched to the child
as these magical versions are to the grown-up reader.

Imagine a world in which
- the sun and the moon follow you when you take a walk;
when you don't move, neither do they.
- the sea water feels the wind churning waves on its surface.
- when the moon disappears from view it has perhaps
gone to see the rain in the clouds, or perhaps it sought shelter
from the cold of the night.
- fish know they are called fish; cows and pigs and grass-
hoppers all know their names.
- clouds are made from chimney smoke from your fire-
place and those of your neighbors.
- people cut up the moon so it should look prettier; first
full, then waxing and waning into crescents and halves.
- the sun is a ball of fire lit by God, who then threw away
the match.
- the clouds are God's breath on cold mornings.
- God is a person who works for children.

For you, this is a world created by a playful imagination.
For your children at Level Two, this world may be the only
world there is, a world constructed by their developing intelligence, the product of serious problem-solving thought.

There is a story from Jewish folklore of two dull-witted
men arguing about when water boils. One maintained it
boiled at 100°C. "But," objected the second, "how does it
know when it has reached a hundred degrees?"

Piaget uses this folk tale to explain how children regard
as living and conscious a large number of objects that for us

are inert. Insofar as things show an activity which is consistent and useful to people, those things must possess a psychic life.

Objects which move must then be alive, must know they are moving and want to move where they do. Sun, stars, and moon journey through the universe at their own discretion. Bicycles, motors, and doors feel their motion and can hurt or help you independent of what you do with them.

A child might then replace a half-buried stone dislodged by her foot so that it doesn't suffer from being moved. Considerate of their feelings, she brings home several pebbles or flowers so that they can have company and not be lonely. Perhaps she moves stones from one side of the path to the other, so they won't always have to look at the same view. (Sully/Piaget.)

A man recalls a childhood encounter with a window that fell shut suddenly, nearly guillotining him:

> "I was fascinated by the window which I had seen moving by itself like a person and even quicker than I could. I was certain it had wanted to do me harm and for a long while I never came near it without experiencing feelings of fear and anger." [Michellet/Piaget.]

We have all seen children get mad at toys and doors for hurting them, slapping back at the objects they see as causing their pain. Even grown-ups have been known to curse and kick unhearing and inanimate things as they trip over tables, bruise themselves on the corners of bed frames, and put money in vending machines which give them nothing in return.

Endowing objects with will and the ability to move about on their own is called animism: animating the inert, granting life to the inanimate, and attributing human consciousness and will to things that operate according to other laws of motion.

Children's questions about the world (Who made the sun?

Why do we have dreams? Why is grass green? Where is the baby now that Aunt Ellen will have next summer?) see a purpose for all things. Animism locates these purposes in the things themselves. But purpose, even if it were to inhere in everything always, can alternatively be located in the creator of those things. Then the creator, be it God or mortal, constructs both natural and manufactured objects alike: by artifice. Piaget calls this way of looking at the world as if it were manufactured like factory goods "artificialism." For children beginning to explore the causes of things and events, the hows and whys behind the whats and wheres, artificialism, like animism, appears to offer solutions: The sun is a ball of fire God tosses in the sky above San Francisco from behind the East Bay hills; the men of Chicago dug Lake Michigan so that the local people might have beaches to visit; and babies are manufactured by people as if they were automobiles, TV sets, or dolls. A Level Two child knows that babies have not always existed, they must be built.

Jane, age four, told me: "To get a baby to grow in your tummy, you just make it first. You put some eyes on it. Put the head on, and hair, some hair all curls. You make it with head stuff you find in the store that makes it for you. Well, the mommy and daddy make the baby and then they put it in the tummy and then it goes quickly out."

A year earlier, she had asked her mother, "How do you make babies?" Listening to her mother's long, scientific explanation, she looked bored. Fascinated by the bellies of pregnant women, she pointed them out on the street and asked how the babies get out. While clear about the location of babies before birth and the exit through which they enter the world, she puzzled about the process: The baby belongs to its parents, who wish for and arrange its arrival. It is still the all-powerful parents who must make the baby. But how? Why, like anything else that is made by people, by getting all the ingredients and mixing them together, gathering the components and assembling them to construct a finished product. At this early stage, children seem to feel no difficulty in thinking of things and beings as, at the same time, living and artificially made. Even without the "bionic" heroes that further confound the issue.

According to four-year-old Laura, "When people are already made, they make some other people. They make the bones inside and blood. They make skin. They make the skin first and then they make blood and bones. Maybe they just paint the right bones. They paint the blood, paint the red blood and the blue blood." When asked how babies start to be in mommies' tummies, she replied: "Maybe from people. They just put them in the envelope and fold them up and the mommy puts them in her 'gina and they just stay in there." When asked where the babies were before they were in the envelope, she answered, "They buy them at the store."

Similarly, Tom, a four-year-old boy, suggested that a woman who wants a baby should "maybe get a body . . . at the store"; she could then "put it all together" with "tools" to "produce a baby." Although his mother reported that he had received no religious training, Tom attributed a major role in the theater of creation to God. According to Tom, God makes mommies and daddies "with a little seed": "He puts it down . . . on the table . . . then it grows bigger. The people grow together. He makes them eat the seed, then they grow to be people. Then they stand up and go some place else, where they could live. The seed makes them into people. Before, they were skeletons. At God's place."

Clearly, making mommies and daddies is harder than making babies. A woman who knows the best places to shop and has minimal mechanical skills can assemble a baby. But to create anything as complicated as an adult requires supernatural powers.

These children seem undeterred by the fact that they've never seen a baby factory or a rack of diapered infants at the local supermarket. When provoked by curiosity or directly questioned, they simply make up answers, fitting what they have been told and what they have seen into their way of looking at the world. Because children at this level believe that everything in the world has been made either by a magicianlike God or by people, they assume that babies are created in a similar way.

These children are still egocentric; they can interpret the world only in terms of events or processes they have themselves experienced. Therefore, they often fall into the digestive fallacy and believe that babies are conceived by swallowing and born by elimination. Especially if they believe that the baby grows in the mother's "tummy," children base their theories of the baby's entrance and exit on their knowledge of their own bodies: Anything that is in their tummies must first have entered through their mouths and will eventually leave their bodies when they go to the toilet.

A friend remembers patiently explaining the "facts of life," including intercourse and conception, to her six-year-old son, only to hear him mutter to himself as he walked away from this briefing session, "But I know she really swallows it." Tom talked about God making the skeletons "eat the seed" to become people, and before Laura decided the baby gets into the mommy when "they put them in the 'gina" she suggested that "they just eat them."

Nursing and its role in nourishing the growing baby intrigues young children. Breasts and milk can overshadow the less-witnessed and less-visible aspects of childbearing. When I asked five-year-old Lisa how a woman might get a baby to begin to grow inside her, she replied, "Get some milk in her titties." "How would she do that?" I asked. "Get some milk and just drink it." Tom, when asked the same question, suggested that the baby "eat the mommy's milk."

For many children, it is her having breasts that enables the mother to grow babies. Daddies don't grow babies, in Lisa's words, "because the daddy doesn't have bigger titties, and the mom does."

To eat is to grow, for young children. They are urged

to eat nourishing food so that they will "grow up big and strong . . . like Daddy and Mommy." We saw that at Level One children said that people get to be parents by "eating vegetables" and "growing up." If you eat, you will grow, and your size is dependent upon how much you have eaten. Jill explained, "My daddy is bigger than my mommy because he ate too much. If my mommy ate too much, then she's going to be bigger than my daddy." So, at Level Two, the baby must eat to grow and the mother may have to eat something to begin the baby's growth. She must also eat in order to gain the necessary size and strength to be a mother. I asked Lisa how mommies get to be mommies:

LISA: From God.

ME: When do they start to be mommies?

LISA: From their mothers. They're babies, then they're little children, then they grow up to be mothers.

ME: Do they have to do something besides grow up to be a mother?

LISA: Yeah. Eat a lot of food, and don't get no cavities, and I guess have fun.

ME: Anything else?

LISA: Yeah, get a lot of energ, enerd, energy.

If the baby begins by its mother's eating, then it may pass through her digestive tract to exit in the toilet, like everything else that passes through the human body. This belief in birth as elimination is not uncommon among young children, based as it is on their knowledge of their own bodies.

"The baby comes out of a place in your fanny," said Sally. Confusion as to where the baby emerges persists even when there has been accurate education. Two five-year-old boys discussed the location from which the baby emerges:

ALLAN: It comes out somewhere *near* the vagina, but not really.

JERRY: They come out of their tush [anus].

ALLAN: No, not the tush. It's somewhere near the tush, but not the tush.

It is difficult to be certain about something you have never seen. Even when the mental image is clearer, the child may wonder, as did six-year-old Adam: "You know what's funny? How could something big like a baby come out something small like a vagina?" It seems like magic.

Other ways out may appear more likely. Children often think of the baby as coming out the belly button, the only way it could emerge directly from the "stomach." This curious knob or cranny must have a purpose, a purpose they correctly associate with babies and birth, and it is the only potential opening in the belly itself.

Even children who haven't heard about Caesarian births come to the conclusion that surgery may be the only way to extricate the infant from the abdomen. The baby is so much bigger than the body's natural openings that a new opening must be needed. Four-year-old Carol told me: "They go to the doctor and the doctor cuts your stomach. I know all about babies." Her mother then told her that she had not been cut out. When I later asked her how she had been born, she changed her story. "I fell out," she said, "the baby falls out, right out." "That would be nice," her mother added.

Sometimes the doctor need not resort to such drastic measures. Five-year-old George said, "Maybe one day Mommy had a hole in her stomach and my brother got out when she went to the hospital, and the man sewed her up with some sticky stuff." "The doctor pulls the baby out, from here," said Sam, pointing to the center of his abdomen. "They go to the hospital," explained Alex, talking of mothers. "And they open up their legs, and the doctor takes it out. From here," he said, indicating his crotch. When questioned further, these children seemed to say that however much the events they describe challenge their logic and the evidence of their senses, the power of the doctor explains everything: "The doctor can do those things."

Seldom does their image of birth center around a passive infant moved along the birth canal by the muscular contractions of its mother. Alex talked about the baby "crawling" through the tummy and out between the legs. Sometimes the imagery grows more violent. "I punched my mommy. I was inside her and I punched the things that was around me and all my water came out. I growed in a little egg in there and then I popped out," explained Jerry. Darryl volunteered, "I know how they get out—they have to fight to get out."

Mark's account of birth was more peaceful, but retains the perspective of the active infant: "The baby grows and gets bigger and then pops out. I don't really mean pop, I mean push. It starts pushing, then sort of winds out, sort of relaxes and sinks out."

Carol, at four, was present at a home birth. She described what she saw: "Born means the baby comes out of the stomach. The doctor comes over your house, and he tells you if you want to have your baby today, someday, and they say yes or no. If they say yes, then the doctor will get it out. You have to push really hard and you have to breathe. You have to keep your body down, not your legs. You have to lie down on your bed, and you need a lot of towels. You have to push really hard while someone's holding your legs. That helps the baby come out. And the doctor's helping you. He tries to get your baby out. He gets all his tools to do that. Yeah, he has some funny scissors and some . . . it's if you cut yourself, it doesn't hurt. And so it's really hard to have a baby. There's a daddy, too. He helps the doctor and you get the baby out. He gets some cottons for the baby, so the blood won't come on the bed. But you need something on you after you have the baby. Because all blood is coming out, and you need to stay in bed for a few days. Because when you're getting up that will help not all the blood come out." Following the birth, she and her three-year-old friend, the older sister of the baby whose birth she described, played at giving birth. In their play they reenacted the powerful scene they had witnessed, this time as active participants, mothers birthing their own infants.

Parents who told me their children knew "everything" about how people get babies would be surprised to hear the stories their offspring told me. We have seen how children can become confused in thinking about what mothers do to get babies and how those babies actually are born. Paternity is still more difficult for the child to comprehend. What do men do to contribute to the growth, or at this level the production, of babies?

Most of the children at this level are clear that a daddy doesn't carry the developing infant in his body. And their explanations for why this is so take into account either physiology or social role. According to Karen, daddies don't grow babies because there would be no way out for the fully developed fetus: "Daddies don't have a hole where the babies come out." Their inability to nurse is another often-repeated reason for why males don't become pregnant. Alex, however, based his explanation solely on reasons of social role: "Because sometimes they have to work and it might come out when they're working, and they'll have to work with it in the tummy. But when there's a baby in the tummy, they have to go to the doctor right away, see. So they don't grow babies." When I asked him whether dads have something to do with the getting of babies, he replied: "I don't know. I think so." "What?" I asked. "They have to find a witch to tell them to turn them into a girl. If they're a girl, she'll know how to get a baby."

Although the magic is seldom this explicit, many children's explanations of paternity depend on fantastic manipulations beyond the realm of the possible. A child who asked her mother how she got in her belly was told "Well, Dad put you in there." She then assumed that he had opened her mother's body and stuck her in, wrapping a fully formed infant in a maternal cover. She didn't know why she had to stay there for a while, except perhaps so she wouldn't get "chilly cold."

Many of these children were adamant that "you need a man and a woman to make a baby" without having any real clarity about the man's contribution. When I asked four-year-old Allan what the man does, his answer reflected the opacity of the concepts involved: "He has something that's like an X-ray, and he uses the X-ray to look inside himself, to see if he has what he needs inside himself to make a baby with." Somewhere in the mysterious caverns of his body, invisible to the naked eye, some unknown ingredient lingers. Perhaps.

At Level Two, many children puzzle over how the seeds get from point of origin to destination. Even when they have been given the facts, they have trouble creating mental images of what they themselves have not seen. And because the truth may be discomforting—the only analogy children commonly have for penetration is their own experience of "getting a shot"—they may try to account for the transfer of genetic materials in other ways. "The father just lies in bed," Carol told me, "until the mother goes to sleep. And then the sperm comes out and comes in the mother."

Sharon had been told that the daddy puts the seed into the mommy on her egg, that the egg and seed form into one piece and grow into a baby in the mommy's womb until it's big enough to come outside and live. So she knew that an egg and a seed are involved in making babies, but she had not been told about how the seed gets to the egg. When I asked her how people get babies, she replied:

SHARON: From marrying people. They put seeds in their vaginas. The mommies open up their tummy, but sometimes they open up their vaginas. So the daddies, so they can put their eggs in them, and they can put the seeds in them.

ME: Who puts the eggs in them?

SHARON: The daddies do.

ME: Are seeds and eggs the same thing or different things?

SHARON: They're different things. An egg is bigger than a seed. And it has a shell. A seed is something that's round, and it's too much small, and it grows people.

ME: What do the egg and the seed have to do with getting babies?

SHARON: Well, the egg has to be on the seed. And then it grows a baby.

ME: Can an egg grow to be a baby without a seed?

SHARON: No . . . 'cause it has to be a special kind of egg and a special kind of seed. The seed is not a growing seed, but a baby seed, it grows babies. It's in daddies' tummies. Eggs are in mommies. And I have eggs in my tummy.

ME: If the seed is in the daddy, how does it get on the egg?

SHARON: When the daddy gets it. I don't know how exactly, 'cause he can't really open up all his tummies. Maybe it rolls out. I think the daddy gets it. He puts his hand in his tummy. Then he puts it on the bottom of the mommy, and the mommy gets the egg out of her tummy, and puts the egg on top of the seed. And then they close their tummies, and the baby is born.

For her, the seed and the egg can come together only by manual means. She expressed some doubts that her version of the story could be accurate (" 'cause he can't really open up all his tummies") but her experience provides her with no real alternatives.

Barry had been told that Daddy plants a seed in Mommy that has to grow for a long time; this seed becomes the baby, which is born through a special passageway in Mommy. He told me: "One thing I know, how babies are born, that first of all you, they form from a seed in the uterus. It sort of forms in the shape of a baby. It grows and gets bigger and then pops out. Daddies ask the wife if she wants a baby, and then they get a seed and put it in. He gets the seed somehow when he's born. The daddy plants the seed like a flower, I think, except you don't need dirt. He sticks it in the vagina. I think the baby falls out of the seed, and it just cracks open."

Taking the agricultural metaphor very literally, he described the planting of the seed as something the daddy must do with his hands, " 'cause the mommy can't reach back to the uterus, to the vagina. I mean she can't reach her arm back." He then thought about that some more and changed his mind: "No, I think she could, she probably could." This ended the interview about how people get babies, however, for he then said that he would like to look at pictures, for "that will probably be easier than thinking." Having decided that the mommy can reach her arm to her vagina, he could not find a reason for the involvement of the father. He remained the seed donor, but there was no longer a rationale for his active participation.

Although they may describe the seeds and eggs with which parents make babies as "special" and "just for growing babies," these children's images remain concrete. Eggs look like those in the refrigerator, and seeds resemble those sown in the garden, with which they may even be interchangeable. Selma Fraiberg recalls a "certain literal-minded fellow of six who was led into minor delinquency by the hopes engendered in him" by the information that "the daddy plants the seed." "He stole a package of cucumber seeds from the dime store and planted them (package and all) under a telephone pole 'so's me and Polly can have a baby next summer.'"

Even children who have learned that the male's material contribution to the baby is called *sperm* are not at all sure what the word means or what the thing referred to does. Carol knew that "sperm comes in fathers and eggs come in mothers." When I asked her what sperm do, she said: "Sperms? You put them in your mama's body and then you look in the telescope. After the sperm comes in then it touches the eggs where the baby are." She had probably seen the sperm described as so small that they can be seen only under a microscope. Their purpose eluded her.

Ellen believed that the sperm were somehow involved in getting the baby out: "The doctor takes the baby out of my mama's belly with a sperm. The sperms help you come out from the belly. The baby goes through the vagina and goes into the sperm, and the doctor takes it out. The sperms swim and then get in. They have to catch to the egg. They have to swim and then they have to hit the egg. They have to catch the eggs because there's babies in it, in the big belly, and the big people have to go to the big hospital to have a baby. Then the baby comes out and you live with it." Although Ellen did not include sexual intercourse in her description, or even identify the sperm as coming from the father, the role in which she cast the sperm was the same as for Laura, who did both.

Laura told me: "A boy sticks the penis into a girl and then the sperm goes in, the sperm goes into the egg and makes a baby. The sperm goes round the egg. Then it gets big and then the baby comes out." When I asked her to tell me more about the sperm, her account became more confused: "The sperm can make a baby come out. It's like from a frog. It has these [drawing squiggly lines in the air with her fingers] things that can make them swim around the egg. And it has a little head. An egg is a little thing that helps people out. It helps chickens. You can eat chicken eggs and birds' eggs, and babies come out of the birds' eggs." "Is the egg that people babies come from like chicken eggs or is it different?" I asked. "It's different, 'cause it's just round. Chicken eggs are like this," she explained, drawing an oval in the air. "What about the egg and the sperm coming together makes a baby?" I continued. " 'Cause the mother wants to make a baby," she concluded.

Karen, too, saw the father's role as helping to liberate an encapsulated baby already formed in the mother: "Well, the dad gets on top of the mother and puts the penis into the mom's vagina. And then it helps the baby come out. It helps the mom get the baby out." Here it is the penis, not the sperm, that permits the baby to leave the mother's body, perhaps by enlarging the pathway.

A creation myth of the Djanggawul tribe of Australian aborigines takes a similar view of the male role in procreation. Their original ancestors, they believe, were a Brother and Sister. The Brother put his index finger in his pregnant Sister's vagina. Then he pulled it away. At the same time a

baby boy came out. Sister was careful to open her legs only
a little, for if she spread them, children would have flowed
from her, as she kept many people stored away in her
uterus.

For four-year-old Janet, the father's role was one of pro-
tecting the fragile fetus. When I asked her how a daddy gets
to be a daddy, she said: "He fucked and the sperms went in,
to save the egg, so it won't get cracked. The sperm goes in
to protect the eggs. It swims, I think, just like little fishes.
So something bumpy won't crack the eggs." She went on to
describe how this happens: " 'Fuck' means get on top of
each other. And then the things grows and grows and grows
and grows and then they get pregnant and then it comes
out the vagina. The sperm swims in—into the penis—and
then it, I think it makes a little hole, and then it swims into
the vagina. The sperm has a little mouth to dig a hole." For
her, the sperm is a small animal; if it has a head, then it
must have a mouth, and the ability to burrow its way purposefully to its destination.

Like most of the children at Level Two who described intercourse, Janet was not explicit as to how it occurred, but
was very clear that it was for procreation only. "They do it,"
she told me, "when they want a baby they do it, but when
they don't want a baby they don't do it." Getting the penis
into the vagina, pushing the sperm out through the penis,
and having it burrow into the mother, seems so difficult and
complicated that it would be foolish to go to all that trouble
when you don't get anything as valuable as a baby in return.
Another four-year-old attested to the intricacy of this pro-
cedure by guessing that "it must have been Saturday or Sun-
day to take the time to do it." That the sexual act can be
one of love and pleasure is difficult for children to understand. Their own experience cannot correct the frequent
impression that penetration may be painful and coitus an
aggressive act. Selma Fraiberg tells a story of a six-year-old
questioning her mother about the imminent birth of the
family's third child: "Katie said, 'Mother, can some mothers

and daddies try to have a baby and not get one?' 'That's right,' said her mother. 'Gee, aren't we lucky in our family,' Katie said. 'Every time you and daddy tried we got a baby!' ' "

Although they may not spontaneously conclude that sexual intercourse is making love, a pleasureful expression of affection and closeness, children do seem able to absorb direct information that this is so. Karen told me, "They would do that if they didn't want a baby and they would do that if they wanted a baby." "Why," I asked, "would they do that if they didn't want a baby?" "Because," she said, "they want to hug each other."

Many of the children insisted that parents had to be married to have a baby, sometimes directly contradicting parents who told them that while marriage may be desirable it is not necessary to be married to have a baby. "I have to get married, so I can get a baby," Sharon told me. When I asked her why, she had no answer. Karen, too, insisted that "if you want a baby you have to get married. First you get married and then you go on a honeymoon." When asked what about marrying started the baby, she said, "the part when the father sticks his penis in the vagina. But," she added, "they would do that if they weren't married."

Janet's insistence on marriage was more adamant. "If they get a baby, they have to get married," she told me. "Because that's the way you get milk." "How does getting married give you milk?" I asked. " 'Cause then the milk . . . 'cause then the man who put the medicine in won't let you keep your baby. The man who took the baby out." The doctor, who delivers the baby and gives the mother medicine to contract her uterus, enforces social convention by impounding babies whose mothers aren't married. Her concern about social convention is a precursor of the preoccupation with roles and rules that characterizes the next level.

Sometimes children generalize from their own family history to the world at large. Two little girls who didn't remember their mother's first husband remember her second wedding as an important event in their own young lives.

They were four and six and a half at the time, and very excited to be part of the ceremony. Later, their mother watched as they played with their Barbie dolls. Each time the Barbie dolls would go out and get two children and then go on to marry. To have a wedding without the children being present would be an act of deprivation, barring them from an important family occasion.

"When they get married" is often given as the answer to questions of how mommies and daddies get to be mommies and daddies. Definitions of what a parent is have become more categorical at this level, and adults are seen as having to do something in order to become parents. A mommy "is a girl that takes care of little children" or "who baby-sits, no, who takes care of you." Mommies get to be mommies, said George, because they "growed and growed and growed, by eating. Then their head grows on and then their eye grows on, and then their other eye gets on, and then their arm gets on, and then their foot gets on." If they then have no children, they are not mommies but "just reg'lar people." Before they can be mothers, explained Noah, "they have to cook, they have to teach school, and they have to learn how to drive a car," all necessary skills for motherhood. When asked how come they had the particular mothers they do, most children answered, like Karen, " 'Cause she's a mommy and I got borned into her tummy." Tom, however, was more fatalistic: "That's the only one God could find."

Daddies, too, are defined by their relationship to their children. "A daddy is a man who takes care of us," Alex said. "A little boy grows up and he's called a daddy," but only "if he had children, like me and my sister." She has the father she does, said Jane, "because Mommy just wanted him." "All the time daddies grow up and then they be child's daddies," explained Carol. "They just tell the mommies that they want to be their daddies." Her daddy was hers "because I wanted to have a daddy and he gets me." When asked why her mother's new mate was not her daddy instead, she replied, "Well, because I want to have a friend."

Because biological paternity is more difficult to understand than maternity, fathers still get to be related by wishes that always come true, even after mothers are seen as assigned by necessities of the flesh.

The paternal tie can feel like a tenuous one. I asked Julie, whose parents had recently separated, how her father started to be her father. "He's not any more though," she told me. "He's not my daddy any more, he moved." "He's still your daddy, even if he doesn't live here," I said. "No, he isn't," she insisted, "he's just going to come back home lots of days to stay while." If a daddy is someone who takes care of children, then a daddy who doesn't is no daddy at all. When biological paternity is still unknown, or only vaguely understood, fatherhood consists of living with and caring for children.

In asking children about the origin of babies, I elicited some stories about the origin of the human species. "Do you want to know how the first people came here?" Allan asked me. "Sure," I replied. "They just, the monkeys turned into people." "How did that happen?" I asked. "I don't know," he admitted, "but it probably was a surprise for the monkeys. Because"—he laughed—"when they had eggs, instead of monkeys, people came out."

Laura went even further back into prehistory to account for human origins. I asked her how mommies get to be mommies. "Well," she said, thoroughly confusing me for a while, "it starts out to be a plant, and then it grows and grows and then it comes into a person." "A plant grows to be a person?" I wasn't sure I had heard right. "Yes." "How does that happen?" "I don't know," she answered, "but my mama told me it." Later, when I asked her how daddies get to be daddies, I figured out what her mother had said. "They grow up to be a plant," she repeated, "and then they grow up to be a person." "When were they a plant?" I asked. "I think after the dinosaurs were dead. First there was fire in the sky. Then fire fell down and maked rocks. And then the plants growed. And then the plants started out to be persons." "How?" "The plant must have magic in his body," she said, wide-eyed, marveling at a story so fantastic that it must involve the supernatural.

Alex told me the biblical story of creation. I had asked him how mommies get to be mommies, but he found the question too narrow, using it only as a point of departure: "They're in another mommy's tummy, and they grow. And the first people in the world is Adam and Eve. And they ate an apple that God told them not to eat. And God's the one who made the world. And factories make some things, and men make things. But God made the factories and the men made the things in the factories. And you know what? Adam and Eve were the first people that grew. And they could eat any food in the world, but not this tree, because it had apples. And then, they eat one. And they'll become all naked, and they'll *know everything,* like God, and they'll know how to build things. And people. And so, God told them not to eat it, and they did. And then God got so mad he sent them out of the pretty garden. And before, before every time, God was always on the world. And there was nothing. Just darkness. All around. God was all alone, and he decided something: that he was going to build the world. That's the end of my story."

A true artificialist, Alex saw God as the manufacturer who started it all. A little confused about who makes what, his division of labor between God and man seems to hinge on the size of the products involved. Anything as big as a factory must be made by God Himself, while their contents are within the capacities of mere mortals. Yet when people, through their transgression, know all that God knows, they too can build other people.

Talking with Level One Children

In the previous chapter, we discussed how to talk with the child who does not yet know that babies grow inside their mother's body. This knowledge, like other ideas new to children, may not be absorbed all at once. Images of babies bought in stores or hospitals may linger. The child can be gently led to examine his belief, to evaluate it and exchange it for a more accurate one. In this section we will explore how to talk with the Geographer, the Level One child.

For example, a child may let you know that he believes that babies are bought in stores.

PARENT: I can see how you might think that babies are bought in stores. Most of the new things we get are bought at the store. But people are very special. People don't buy and sell other people. Can you think of another way people might get babies?

CHILD: You get them at the hospital that gives them to you.

PARENT: Mommies come home from the hospital with their new babies. So the hospital is a place where something important happens for the baby. How do you think the hospital gets the babies?

CHILD: They just have them there. The nurses have them, and the doctors have them.

PARENT: The nurses and the doctors help the mommy and daddy get the baby. But where do you think the baby was *before* it was at the hospital?

CHILD: In another place.

PARENT: Yes, in another place, a very special place just for growing babies. The place is called a uterus, and it's inside the mommy's body, right here [pointing]. So, the mommy has the baby inside her body when she goes to the hospital, and the nurses and doctors help the baby come out.

We have seen that young children have difficulty understanding how "something big like a baby can come out something small like a vagina." They may ask to see the place where the baby comes out. Seeing mother's vagina will not help them understand what they want to know, and she may handle this situation by simply telling them that there are parts of her body that she prefers not to show them.

They can be told that the vagina stretches to allow the baby to pass through. Stretching a rubber band can illustrate the principle.

Once firmly established at Level One, children still believe that babies have always existed. While they may know that babies grow in their mothers' bodies and exit through the vagina, their thinking is in terms of the baby's whereabouts and not its origin. The next step is for them to learn that a baby has a beginning, and that people must take action to start a baby.

While parents would not want to offer the more-flamboyant metaphors that characterize the Level Two child's accounts of the construction of babies as a craft, children's own thinking is developing in the direction of people and/or God making everything and everybody in the world. Not wanting to tell children accounts of birth and conception that are untrue, parents would not want to talk of putting bones and blood together with curls and eyes to make a baby. But in speaking of putting sperm and ovum together to make a baby, they use a way the child can understand to present accurate information.

Let us say that your child has noticed that a neighbor is pregnant. You have talked together about how the baby is growing inside her body. Now, perhaps, your child turns to you and asks: "Where did Ellen get the baby?" By asking a *where* question, she indicates that her current views are at Level One.

Speaking in Level Two terms, you might say: "Only people can make other people. To make a baby person, you need two grown-up people, a woman and a man, to be the baby's mommy and daddy. The mommy and daddy make the baby from an ovum in the mommy's body and a sperm from the daddy's body."

The question of what language to use is important. We have seen that young children are very literal-minded; each word conjures up an image of a real object. They assimilate what they are told to their own experience of the world.

When they hear the word *egg,* they visualize chicken eggs in the refrigerator or on their plates. When they hear the word *seed,* their minds wander to planting time in the garden or eating watermelons or pumpkins. Lonnie Barbach writes of a friend who had learned "at the age of five that babies came from an egg in the Mommy's tummy that Daddy fertilized. For years she carried around the mental image of Daddy shoveling manure on a chicken egg sitting on Mommy's tummy."

Even if they don't fully understand what a sperm or an ovum is, and they won't, there is less chance of confusion when parents talk about sperm and ova than when they attempt to simplify by speaking about seeds and eggs. It is especially tricky to speak of ova, because the Latin rule for forming the plural (one ovum, many ova) is so different from the English. Personally, I think that bad Latin is better for children than thinking that they grow from eggs with shells laid by a bird. Remember three-year-old Alan, who said to his mother, "If Daddy put his egg in you, then I must be a chicken."

If speaking of ova is awkward for you, referring to the ovum as an "egg cell" and not simply as an "egg," describing how the two differ, will help clear up the confusion.

Because sperm and ovum are new words, they require explanation. For example: "Sperm and ovum are little things in people that are specifically for making babies. Daddies' bodies make sperm, and mommies' bodies make ovums. You need one sperm and one ovum to make a baby." If the child is curious to know more, age is no reason to avoid presenting how sperm and ovum get together.

5

The In-Betweens— Level Three

Level Three children range in age from five to ten. They may know that three major ingredients go into making babies: social relationships such as love and marriage, sexual intercourse, and the union of sperm and ovum. However, their ability to combine these factors into a coherent whole is limited. These children are in a transitional period between the stages of development that Piaget calls *preoperational* and *concrete operational*.

A preoperational child builds mental maps based on her own experiences; she solves problems by intuition. She cannot assign objects to categories. Asked to define an apple, she's likely to say, "It's to eat." As she moves into the next stage, which can happen any time between seven and ten years old, she learns to think systematically and generally about concrete objects. Ask her about an apple now and she'll say, "It's a fruit."

During this transitional period, children are aware that some parts of their explanations don't quite jibe with others. Their accounts of procreation are a mixture of physiology and technology, but they are more insistent than Level Two children that the operations involved be technically possible. Gone are the steps in manufacture that common experience can readily disprove.

Yet some magical thinking remains. Because ejaculation

is as yet outside their experience and fertilization will forever be invisible (except perhaps in *National Geographic* documentaries), these concepts remain elusive, susceptible to infiltration by "supernatural" ideas. They may believe that for sperm and ovum to come together, some manual, medical, or magical intervention is necessary. When the rudiments of sexual intercourse are known, most insist that people would go to all that trouble only when they want a baby.

Because their thinking is still very literal, they are apt to misinterpret metaphors. A sperm described as "looking like" a tadpole may be seen as a separate and complete little animal that can make decisions and move where it wishes. "Planting a seed," a euphemism favored by many parents, may require manually sowing the seed. Love may be as essential an ingredient in babymaking as flour is in baking a cake, and marriage may not only be necessary for reproduction, but sufficient. For many children at this level, social conventions are as inexorable as physical laws.

By the time a child is at Level Three, the Age of Reason has begun. Intellectual activity started far earlier, with the toddler's manipulation of objects in play, the questions children rain on their parents, and the fanciful theories they create to explain how everything works and why.

To question, children need only be curious. To invent solutions, they draw on their imaginative ability. It is only when they attempt to verify those solutions, to hold them up to the measure of experience and opinion, that reason is required. Reasoning is the work of controlling and proving hypotheses, thinking to discover the truth rather than for the pure delight of creation. And, true to the developmental insight of the Catholic Church, children typically begin to reason at about seven.

The need to reason does not arise spontaneously. It is not for ourselves that we work so hard to verify our statements. We do so because other people leave us no choice. Objectivity, as commonly understood, has as its principal criterion the agreement of different minds. Left to our own devices as individuals, we would immediately believe our own ideas are the sum total of reality.

Experience alone does not always rectify beliefs; things are in the wrong, not the children who conceived them as different in fancy than they are in fact. If a mason can build a brick wall and a laborer dig a ditch, why might men not build mountains and oceans? The child, who does not work, has little experience with the resistance of objects. In play, things can be what they wish them to be.

Before they are seven or eight, children have a hard time telling the difference between physical causality and psychological or logical motivation. They don't know that their thoughts do not exist as real events outside their heads. Convinced that adults are their superiors, they cannot imagine that adults might not understand everything they say and know their thoughts before they voice them. Even a child who knows that dreams are subjective, so that she will deny that someone else can touch or see her dreams, may say that the dreams take place in the room in front of her.

Children's thought is egocentric. Untutored in the art of entering into other people's points of view, they cannot imagine any perspective other than their own. Jimmy may insist, for example, that while he has a brother named Michael, Michael has no brothers.

The same obstacles that prevent children from adapting themselves to other people's points of view are at work to prevent their using the evidence of their own senses to construct a coherent world view. They take their own immediate perceptions as something absolute. They do not analyze what they perceive, but merely throw the new in with previously acquired and ill-digested material. Sometimes they see objects and events not as they really are but as they would have been imagined if the child had been asked to describe them before looking at them.

Alert, curious explorers of a fresh, new world, children observe masses of detail. Having no organizing principle, they have difficulty in thinking about more than one thing at a time. So they squander data rather than synthesizing it into packages that can be stored and retrieved intact.

Children's drawings are a good example of how they depict reality to themselves. Pictures of tables, trees, and people are not faithful copies of the objects themselves. But this is not because they are technically unskilled as artists. Instead of looking at an object and trying to reproduce it, children draw only what they already know about things, copying their own mental pictures. A landscape requires grass, trees, and sky; the grass must be on the bottom, the sky on top, and the trees rest flatly on the grass; a house may float in the center of the paper.

It is hard for children before seven or eight years of age to grasp the relations of the whole to its parts. Like "all the king's horses and all the king's men," young children cannot put parts back together again into the wholes they were before being broken down into their elements. But their grab bags of juxtaposed judgments unconnected by any coherent bond does not lead to feelings of chaos or discontinuity. Instead, in the child's mind everything is connected to everything else.

Their early judgments do not imply each other but simply follow one upon the other. "And then . . . and then . . . and then," the child's narrative of explanation typically goes, stringing together events without "because" or "although" or "despite," moving from particular to particular without appeal to general propositions. Simplifying and fusing a mixed bag of elements, children retain an unquestioning belief that their condensed versions of reality are the way things are.

Judgments strung together without synthesis act one at a time. Up to age seven or eight, thought teems with contradictions. Boats float "because they're light," so that the strong water holds them up, while in the next sentence a "big boat" is said to float "because it's heavy" and, presumably, strong enough to support itself. Given a complex prob-

lem, children shift from one approach to another in a series
of attempts. But they cannot reconstruct the route of their
meanderings from question to solution if asked how they
arrived at their conclusions.

Oblivious to the need for logical justification and unaware
of their own thought processes, children see no need to
reconcile apparent contradictions. Children may move freely
from the egocentric world that has play as its supreme law
to the socialized state that demands shared perceptions.
Neither of these worlds supplants the other for some time.

But children are none the worse for the dual nature of
their reality. They shift comfortably back and forth between
belief and play. Each object exists not only as itself but as
whatever propelled the child to engage with it, so that a
shoebox may remain a shoebox while it serves as a doll's
bed. Which is it *really*? Both.

But these worlds do not remain interchangeable equals
for long. Other people keep insisting that we make sense, that
we share their perceptions of objects and events, and when
we don't, that we back our assertions with evidence. Social
experience gives rise to a desire for system and consistency;
judgment changes and reasoning begins.

At about seven or eight, children begin to make comparisons between play and the reality of everyday life. They
begin to see the other person's point of view, to realize that
if I have a sister my sister must also have a sister, and to
put things together according to how they relate to the
whole in which they partake. They begin to avoid contradicting themselves, wonder about how what's necessary dif-
fers from what's possible, and recognize that chance plays
a role in the turn of events. When everything could be justi-
fied by a reference to anything else, nothing was inexplicable
and chance was neither a necessary nor even a sensible
concept.

These changes in thinking do not happen all at once.
Reasoning is a tricky process. Precausal explanations do not
vanish overnight to be replaced by logical, scientific thought.

Instead, children's growing awareness that there are points of view other than their own begins an overhaul of their old ideas, which are lined up, taken apart, examined for coherence and communication value, and reassembled. Level Three is a time of conceptual housecleaning, a time of transition during which old thought patterns mingle with the new.

Children at this level explain procreation as a mixture of physiology and technology, but they stick to operations that are technically feasible. Level Three children know that Mommy and Daddy can't open and close their tummies, but they may assume that conception is impossible without marriage. Social roles and social rules have become an important part of the puzzle of reproduction.

Children at this level of understanding may still believe the world of nature is alive; they talk about nonliving things and those living things that are not whole creatures as if they possessed will and acted purposefully. Ellen, at seven, said: "The sperm is like a baby frog. It swims into the penis and makes a little hole. It bites a hole with its little mouth and swims into the vagina."

They may also take quite literally their parents' explanations of conception as "planting a seed." The "agricultural fallacy" is still prevalent; although at this level the seeds don't come in packets from the hardware store, they may still need to be planted by hand. The transfer of the seed from father to mother may take place at a distance, like the cross-pollination of flowers whose pollen is carried from plant to plant by bees and gusts of wind.

Parents no longer have the variety of ingredients available in the marketplace to help them make babies. They are limited to the contents of their own bodies for materials, although they may have to depend on the doctor to supply the critical ingredient. Younger children may believe that "snakes and snails and puppy-dog tails" or "sugar and spice and everything nice" are recipes for making boys and girls, but now the metaphor of manufacture includes less-fanciful flourishes. Instead of the freedom of the artist to "get some hair all curls" and "paint the red blood and blue blood," we now see only the concrete addition of parts as the baby grows a head and then a leg and then an arm.

As I've said before, children now may know that three major ingredients go into making babies: social relationships, such as love and marriage; sexual intercourse, and the union of sperm and ovum. However, even those who mention all of these are unable to combine these factors into a coherent whole. During this transitional period children are often aware that their explanations don't quite add up. More knowledgeable about adult criteria for "making sense," they may hesitate to guess about things that confuse them.

Children at this level vary considerably among themselves in the weight given to physiological factors in explaining how it is that babies start to develop inside mothers' bodies. Some confine their discussion to social conventions.

"Well, I first thought, when I was seven," said Isabel at eight, "that all you have to do is get married. And then"— her tone became very dramatic—"all you would have to do is read a book, and then you would have a baby." A year later, she was condescending toward the magic of her former belief, but didn't have much with which to replace it. "I never really got around to how people have babies," she explained, "because I have loads of other things to do." Although she didn't really know what being married had to do with getting babies, she insisted that parents have to be married because "they have to like each other a lot, and they have to share the baby."

Isabel knew that babies start to develop nine months before being born, but she said she did not know what happens nine months prior to birth to start the process of development. Her mother claimed that she had read two books that explicitly described the entire reproductive process. Isabel learned from this that to get a baby you must read a book.

She used to think, just one year before, that "if you didn't want to get married and you wanted a baby, all you had to do is just read a book to yourself, that same book I read, and then you'd have it. I don't know what the book would say." Would it matter? "Well, yes, it would matter, but I don't really know what it would say because I don't go to churches and weddings that much."

To Isabel, knowledge is power. You must only learn the secret of birth to realize its contents, a secret of human creation based on social convention and heavenly covenant. According to her mother, Isabel's sex education by two excellent books "seemed to answer all her questions" since "she hasn't asked since." If, when she asked how people get babies, she was handed a book and told to read it, it was no wonder that she thought books were the single most important factor in the getting of babies.

Even when they can offer no explanation of why marriage is helpful in getting babies, most of these children are orthodox adherents of conventional morality. For them, however, this is no mere social contract, but a law of nature, from which deviation is not only terrible but beyond the realm of possibility. Nine-year-old Larry tried to communicate how topsy-turvy the world would be if marriage were optional to childbearing. He wasn't sure why "you have to be married to be a mother or father," but "if you weren't married and you were called a mother, then it would be sort of weird." The skip-rope rhyme so popular with grade-school girls describes a necessary progression: "First comes love, then comes marriage, then comes [name of skipper] with a baby carriage. How many children will she have? One, two, three . . ." The better the skipper, the more children she will eventually bear.

Marriage may be seen as sufficient as well as necessary for getting babies. An older child remembered that every time she asked about babies, the response was always "Well, God gets you the baby when you're married." "I thought it was *so neat*," she recalled, "that God knew that people were married. I thought that it was so neat, like someone could have a baby *right* after she was married almost, and I decided that was so neat. She must be really chosen, and God decided to give her a baby really quickly after she was married. And then when I found out that the man played a part in it, I wanted to punch the people out, because they took the magic out of it, the magic that God blessed you with this nice baby."

There may be material as well as social and spiritual reasons for marriage. For seven-year-old Karl, marriage was the means of obtaining the all-important seed which develops into a baby inside the mother. Fathers get to be fathers when "they and the woman marry," he told me. "And then sometimes they get a baby. No, if they marry, then they usually do get a baby. Marrying gives you the seed."

Children are now more aware of parents', teachers', and friends' attitudes about sexual topics. Unlike their younger brothers and sisters, who typically answer freely and unselfconsciously, they may show considerable embarrassment and even refuse to answer.

It is difficult to know just what seven-year-old Marie thinks about how the baby starts to develop. When I asked her how the baby comes out of the mother, she smiled and explained her smiling by saying " 'cause it's nasty sort of . . . well, it's not nasty but it's hard to tell you." When asked to advise the hypothetical cave-dwellers about how to get a baby, she said: "I would tell them to 'do it' with a man, and then you'd get one. It's hard to tell you what 'do it' means. I don't really know how you get a baby. I only know that you 'do it,' and I don't know if you eat any medicine or something. I don't really know how to really get a baby because my mother never ever told me about it."

Her mother told me that Marie was taught "sperm/egg physiology" and about "intercourse as a function of procreation and a love relationship," but Marie would describe the baby's growth only in terms of size: "How does it start to grow? Well, it comes out. It just grows a tiny bit when it's in the stomach, and then it gets bigger when it's out. The stomach isn't big enough for someone like you, so it can't grow that big. So that when it gets as big as the stomach can make it, then it comes out."

Her brother Frank, one year older, seems to have absorbed more about the "love relationship" than about the "sperm/egg physiology." When asked how his dad got to be his father, he said: "Well, he's a doctor and actually he helped with all the stuff, and he mostly did help." How? "I guess you know. You know I don't like saying it. I have to spell it out to my mommy, because I don't really like saying it."

His considerable embarrassment faded when I suggested he spell to me what he didn't want to say. His tone changed, and he went buoyantly on: "Okay, some people say its p-u-s-s-y, and some people say it's, I don't know the real word for it, but most people say it's f-u-c-k."

What does that mean?

"It's like when people are naked, and they're together, and they just lie together, I guess. Like they're hugging. Some men give hickies, except my dad don't. They're just together."

What does that have to do with getting babies?

"I don't know. I guess it's like mothers and fathers are related, and their loving each other forms a baby. It's just there's love, and I guess it just forms a baby, like I said before. It comes just by loving and stuff. I guess the love forms the beans, and I guess the beans hatches the egg."

Beans? Yes, beans. To find out what the beans are we have to look at his explanation of how the baby starts to be in its mother's body: "Well, I forgot what those things, ovaries or something. Well, there's like beans which shoot out like, and they come to one of like little eggs or something and they hatch." Perhaps he had seen an illustration of the bean-shaped ovary ejecting an egg and visualized the ovary or "bean" moving toward the ejected egg, helping it to "hatch."

So, love forms beans which hatch eggs. The love between the baby's parents is not just an important part of their relationship but part of the substance of the baby itself, the clay from which it is molded. Fathers get to be fathers "because the lady and the man are married, and he becomes the father because he's related to the baby"; he "got related" by getting married. The sexual relationship in marriage starts the baby, but not because the father contributes any actual material to the embryo. Instead, their lovemaking sets in motion the love that will liberate the baby from the egg.

An adult woman I spoke with remembers having beliefs similar to Frank's when she was eight: "I thought love had something to do with it, too. That you fell in love and married. You could only have a baby when you were married, and that wasn't a legal thing, it was a physical thing. And you could only have a baby if you were in love. I remember, I had cousins, and our families were very close. It must have been when I was seven or eight, when Judy's parents were going through a divorce, and she had a three-year-old sister. And I just couldn't understand. I thought, 'Well, gee, they *must* have been in love three years ago. How come they're not in love any more?' "

According to Diane, the father's contribution is more concrete, but how he participates in procreation remains a mystery. I asked her how babies happen to grow inside mothers.

DIANE: That's a pretty hard question to answer. Well, an egg starts to form inside of a mother. And the baby starts to grow inside the egg. Well, the mother and the father, well, like the baby needs to get—if the mother has blue eyes and the father has brown eyes—needs to get the color of its eyes from someone in the family.

ME: Well, if the baby grows from an egg in the mother, how does it get to look like its father, have the same color eyes or hair, or same nose, or something like that?

DIANE: Because of the father's genes, I guess. I don't know how they get in the baby. Maybe some special germs.

Germs are contagious. They spread from person to person through close contact: kissing, talking, sharing a glass. Several children mentioned germs in describing how the father's genetic contribution finds its way to the mother.

But contagion is no less mysterious than conception. Although conceptually as complex, contagion is something the child has experienced, which makes it a more-accessible idea.

The germ theory and other remote-control models of fertilization may arise either from ignorance or from generalizing from the pollination of plants. But these theories multiply the dangers they attempt to skirt by increasing the possibility of accidental impregnation. One woman described the distress this kind of confusion can lead to:

"I'd like to share something from when I was a kid. I come from a different environment, Latin America, a different background, and sex was a taboo subject. I remember believing for a long time that babies could come from sitting in a place where a boy had sat. And I would not sit, in a bus or anyplace, anyplace where a boy was sitting. And then that changed to babies come when you kiss a guy. I must have been eight, maybe nine then. And then I was kissed by a boy, and I was completely frightened, crying about it, screaming about it, and not telling anybody. But crying and crying and sure I was going to have a baby."

Getting babies is a medical enterprise in our culture. Babies come from hospitals. They are delivered by doctors (who used to bring them to your home in their little black bags). Even the fact of pregnancy is typically announced following a visit to a doctor. Small wonder that children borrow concepts like germs and contagion from their own medical experience to explain other, less-familiar medical manipulations.

The doctor is a prominent figure in children's accounts of reproduction and birth. According to Alice, you need three people, from beginning to end, to make a baby: a mommy, a daddy, and a doctor. She told me, "Well, you have to have a man and a woman. And then you have to have a seed, and stuff from the man, and a doctor and a bed. Then they lie down and the stuff goes into the mother. And they have to get the seed and put it in. And then they lie down and get the stuff from the daddy and put it into the mommy. They get the seed from the doctor—or a store, or something like that—I think it's from the doctor, because the doctor has lots of chemicals that help the baby grow." Both the daddy and the doctor must donate materials to make the baby, and the doctor's contribution seems the more central.

ME: How do people get babies?

ALICE: From the daddy. He has something that helps the mommy get the baby. Some sort of medicine. I don't know what it's called, but it's in here. [She pointed to her crotch.] Well, it goes in to some sort of part, I think it's the vagina, and just fixes up and helps around there, and makes it have a baby.

ME: Can she have a baby if that doesn't happen?

ALICE: I'm not sure because my mommy never told me if you really need that stuff from the daddy to make the baby or not. I don't *think* a baby can grow without that. Because I think it fixes up some special part in there. Maybe it loosens things so the baby can get out when it's time. And fixes up, you know, things that are in there might not be situated in the right place. So it takes them and it moves them and fixes it all up.

ME: Is the baby there before that happens?

ALICE: Well, it has to have a seed, and then the baby's inside the teeny-weeny little seed. I don't know where they get the seed, but the doctor puts them in the vagina.

ME: The doctor puts it in the vagina?

ALICE: I think . . . or the daddy. I'm not sure, but maybe the daddy. I don't really know where he gets the seed. Maybe from the doctor.

ME: What's the seed?

ALICE: Well, it's just a little seed that has to have a little baby inside it. Well, they put it in, and then, see, it's the baby. And then the seed grows to be a baby.

ME: What kind of a situation is needed for the seed to become a baby?

ALICE: Well, the man puts his stuff into the mother. And that fixes up some of it. That stuff is not the seed, it's something to help around it.

ME: How come sometimes there's a baby growing inside a woman and sometimes there isn't?

ALICE: The reason why sometimes there isn't is because they don't have the seed in. Or the stuff from the man. And there is a baby growing, because the seed is in there, and they do have the stuff from the man.

ME: Do they get a baby every time the man puts that stuff in?

ALICE: Well, maybe the doctor puts in some more stuff to situate the baby, so it can grow and grow and you know.

ME: How does the man put the stuff in?

ALICE: They lie down and, I don't know if it just squirts out. Maybe the doctor takes it out and puts it in or something. Maybe it just comes out through his penis. Or maybe some other place, 'cause I don't really stare at them all the time. I can't know where everything is. They lie down and they put them together. So in case it just comes out, it goes into the mommy.

ME: Do they do that because they want a baby?

ALICE: Yes.

ME: Would they do that if they didn't want a baby?

ALICE: No. Well, they really have to want a baby to get one, 'cause it's lots and lots of work. If you just do it for nothing, they think, "Well, this is hard work."

ME: Is the work once the baby is already born or before?

ALICE: Well, to get the baby. If I don't want this baby, then why do I do the work to get it?

ME: What's the work?

ALICE: Well, getting them together, and getting the seed, and going to the doctor.

The father's "stuff," working like a handyman, "fixes up" and "helps around," "situates" and moves the baby "to the right place," and expedites its exit. The father also loves the baby, and its mother, for he gets to be a father by marrying her. But it is the doctor who plays the starring role here: He is the source of the seed which comes with a complete baby inside; the mother and father simply provide the appropriate environment for its development. The physician might also be required to get the "stuff" out of the father and into the mother, and he takes the baby out "from the same place it goes in . . . 'cause the mommy wants it out." He is truly indispensable.

Even children who describe sexual intercourse may still find the process mysterious. Ursula, who is eight, described how the father gives "the stuff" for the baby: "Well, he puts his penis right in the place where the baby comes out, and somehow it comes out of there. It seems like magic sort of, 'cause it just comes out. Sometimes I think the father pushes, maybe." But ejaculation was not the only mystery. She was also hazy about what goes where in sexual coupling. When asked if her father did something else besides marry her mother "to help get [you] born," she replied: "He took the part, not his penis but there's another part, two parts, down here, and he took those and then he put them inside. And then the stuff came out, the shell of it. And that's another thing that helped."

So fathers get to be fathers by donating material from their own bodies which contribute to the formation of their children. According to Ursula, there is no baby until the father gives his part, but she was somewhat vague in describing why his contribution is necessary: "Well, the father puts the shell. I forget what it's called, but he puts something in for the egg. If he didn't then a baby wouldn't come. Because it needs the stuff that the father gives. It helps it grow. I think that stuff has the food part, maybe, and maybe it helps protect it. I think he gives the shell part, and the shell part I think is the skin."

She derives her image of an egg from seeing eggs in the refrigerator. She makes a subtle and interesting extension of her observation of social roles in describing the part fathers play in making babies. The father's culturally defined role as protector is extended to his genetic contribution. He is seen as furnishing the protective shell, the outer covering of the egg, which is then transformed into skin, the outer covering of the person.

Ursula described the growth of the embryo as a rather concrete assemblage of parts: "The egg gets bigger and bigger. It just grows and grows until it's a baby. And it starts changing. Like it starts to grow on a leg. And it starts to grow on a hand. And arms. And when the arms and legs are completed, then the hands, and fingers. And then the feet and toes." As in the manufacture of factory goods, each part is completed before another is assembled.

Ursula was one of the first children I talked with to mention birth control. Most of the children at this level or preceding levels understood family size as an expression of parents' wishes that needed no technical implementation. Or, in a more fatalistic vein, a mother had as many children as happened to be inside her, usually stipulated as the number of children currently in the child's own family. Ursula, however, was aware that people can make decisions that determine whether or not babies are begun. When asked if a couple will have a baby "every time the father gives his stuff to the mother," Ursula replied: "Well, they have to decide if they want to have a baby. And if they don't then the father can't give it. But the mother takes the pill if they don't want a baby. The pills make it so there won't be any egg down in here. So nothing can make the egg." While she accurately described how pills work to prevent conception, it is hard to tell from her account why they might be necessary, since the father "can't give his stuff" if they don't want a baby. When I asked her if he might give it anyway, she said, "Even if he gave his stuff, it wouldn't work. But," she added ,"he wouldn't do it."

Carol was clear about the essentials: "It takes two grown-ups to have a child like my sister Penny. And they, well the sperm has to go into the lady to be able to have a baby, 'cause the sperm goes into the egg, and the sperm makes life for the baby." She was a bit evasive at first when asked to describe how the egg and the sperm get together, but she soon went on to describe sexual intercourse, which she called "screwing": "The man and the woman get together in the bed. The sperm and the egg get together when the woman and the man screw. The man puts his whatever-it's-called in the woman's vagina. And then the sperm can wiggle into the egg, and then the egg hatches or something."

"That's the way I learned, and that's the way that people have their children," she replied to my query about why this joining of man and woman, sperm and egg, was necessary. According to her, this takes place when the egg, which contains a preformed baby, has its growth catalyzed by the sperm: "The sperm has the life in it. The egg is for, like the baby is inside the egg, a little something, a seed or something. And then the sperm goes into the seed or something, and the baby develops. The sperm makes life for the baby. It's just, the sperm is like a little thing. It's a squiggily line and it has a circle there. Here's the egg. It has to go right into the egg. There's like a little hole in the egg. It goes into there and then the baby dissolves, I mean, what's that word? . . . starts forming. And in a few months the baby should hatch, when the sperm goes into the baby's body. I don't know how the sperm makes life for the baby. Just that the sperm goes in, and then that the baby turns out nice. And that's how I learned it, and that's how I know it, because I've only read it, only looked at a little bit of how, the human-body book." Carol continually made reference to this informative book, reconstructing its illustrations with finger drawings in the air.

Despite considerable knowledge, Carol's thinking about family size was somewhat unclear. She could think of two reasons why people don't have babies every time they "screw": Either the baby, for unknown cause, dies inside the mother's body or the sperm fails to gain entrance to the egg. People don't "screw" if they don't want a baby, but their wanting and "screwing" may be to no avail if they have already exceeded their quota. Carol, who thought of the baby as preformed in the egg, needing only to be energized by the life-giving sperm, also saw the mother as housing a fixed number of these baby-containing eggs. She explained why her mother was not then pregnant: " 'Cause the lady, when they screw, the lady has the children, as many children as she's going to have, come out of her. Well, not exactly. They don't come out all at the same time, 'cause then they'd be all twins or triples, sixes or something." So she answered only to retract her original reply, substituting nothing in its place. Her picture of menstruation was on the right track but hazy: "All eggs don't grow to be babies. If the sperm doesn't go to the egg, if the person doesn't have a baby, they have permaments. They bleed blood into the toilet when they go to the bathroom, every month. Just because the sperm hasn't touched the egg."

Jason's sole explanation of why intercourse does not inevitably lead to the birth of a baby was that the baby died. Nine years old, he told me: "When the man lets out this seed or something, and it goes into the mother, the woman, it develops into a baby. And then it grows into a baby, and then she gets pregnant, and then she goes into the hospital and she has the baby. Not all the time. Sometimes it dies when it's in the stomach. Maybe it didn't develop right. Sometimes they don't get enough food or something. Maybe the heart didn't develop right. Sometimes the baby dies."

Tamara was also nine when I asked her how people get babies, and she went straight to the basics: "Well, the mother and the father, the husband and the wife fuck, and then about nine, yeah, nine months after that she sort of feels it, and she thinks it's coming."

I never assumed that because a child used a word that she must know the adult usage of that word, be it street language or technical terminology. I asked Tamara to define "fuck." She explained further: "Well, when the penis goes into the vagina. And there's a hole where it should go into.

And then, it's like they put a sperm together and it starts de-, deforming."

Amid the malapropisms—"sperm" for "embryo" and "deforming" for "developing"—her concept of the baby's beginnings emerged. Its formation involved genital contact but no exchange or transfer of genetic materials: "That little sperm is the baby. They make it when they add, when the penis goes into the vagina, they make the sperm. I don't know how exactly. I think it's the man who makes the sperm. And the woman helps, I think. Well, she doesn't give her help, but the vagina helps. Because you need two, of course, to get a baby, but you need two, I think actually it is two to start a sperm. Two people. A man and a woman."

How do they start a sperm?

"Well, I think, but I'm not sure, that the penis goes into the vagina and, well, I think it does something. I was thinking that it might touch something in a body, and then it starts growing a little sperm. Like it might touch some blood, or a blood vein or a bone, well doubtfully a bone, but something around the clitoris. Maybe the sperm comes out from that little thing, near the clitoris. It comes out and it starts. Then I think it might break off, come loose and break off and it stays in that one place, or goes up the stomach."

Despite her considerable knowledge of anatomy, more extensive than that of any of the other children in her age group and most of those older than she, the process was anything but clear. Unlike most of her agemates, she knew that sexual intercourse is for pleasure as well as procreation. When I asked her if people "fuck" if they don't want a baby, she replied: "Well, yeah, one thing like they love each other a lot. And that's known as when you love each other a whole lot. And also some people like doing that." She has told her mother that when she thinks of love she has good feelings in her vagina.

Since she knows that people have sexual contact without reproductive intent, she must also have some notion of why babies do not always result. She knew that there are pills "so you won't have a baby, and also there are pills you can take so you will have a baby." She also had what amounts to a reverse theory of immunity, whereby intercourse becomes effective for reproduction only after an initial exposure: "Well, I think, when you get married, you go on your honeymoon. Well, you don't have to, but you go on a honeymoon, and then you fuck on your honeymoon. Or somewhere around after the honeymoon or something. And that makes it so you've got each other's germs, and then when you do it again you've got a baby. But sometimes you don't do it like for long enough or something like that, and then you don't get a baby. But I know some people that do fuck a lot, and they don't always have babies. Like they've got three children." So, she offered three possible explanations for why each sexual contact does not lead to pregnancy: pills, not having each other's germs yet, or perhaps the would-be parents stop too soon for the penis to "touch," "loosen," or "break off" the "sperm."

Most of the children at this level explain parenthood as a matter of biology or legality. Mothers are mothers because babies grow inside them. Fathers are fathers because they are married to mothers and, perhaps, are needed to start the baby's development. Tamara's explanation of paternity was more inclusive, taking into account the quality of the relationship between adult and child. She first described fathers as getting to be fathers when "they fuck the woman and they've got a child." But then she realized that her stepfather was a real parent to her: "I call my dad 'Dad.' I say 'Hey, Dad, you home?', you know, like that, because he *is* my dad, although he's not the one who fucked my mom and had me." He "*is*" her dad because he loves her and takes care of her, and because he forms a parenting team with her mother.

Another eight-year-old took a philosophical tone in talking about the destiny of biology: "Well, we have this mother because we have to have her, because we came out of her. And when we came out of her we have to settle for her to

be our mother. But I like her." An existentialist, he chose
to affirm what he could not change, asserting his power by
embracing his fate.

Talking with Level Two Children

We can use what we know about Level Three in talking to children whose thinking is now at Level Two. The
Level Two child usually believes that babies are manufactured. His questions will center on figuring out how
construction occurs. He may have doubts about his own
explanations; over time his own experience will lead to
increased awareness of the improbability of certain key
chapters in his story. Perhaps he clings to outmoded beliefs
because he has nothing to put in their stead. As he moves
toward testing the reality of his ideas, he is getting ready to
weed out the technical impossibilities.

Remember four-year-old Jane, who believed that babies
are made from eyes and hair and "head stuff you find in
the store that makes it for you"? And Laura, who suggested
that people make skin and bones and "paint the red blood
and the blue blood"? In talking with these girls, a compli-
ment on their imagination and ingenuity is a good beginning:

"That's an interesting way of looking at things. That's
the way you'd make a doll. You would buy a head and
some hair and put it all together. But making a real live baby
is different from making a doll or a cake or an airplane."

These children can be led to understand that while a factory may have a wide range of components at its disposal,
babymakers have only certain ingredients from their own
bodies as materials. A parent might continue:

PARENT: Mommies and daddies have special things in their
bodies that they use to make babies. Mommies have
tiny ovum and daddies have tiny sperm. When an
ovum from a mommy and a sperm from a daddy join

together, they grow into a baby inside the mommy's body.

Children who still think of eating or elimination when trying to account for how the sperm or ovum gets into the mother's body and how the baby gets out will need help in sorting out the various entrances and exits in female anatomy. Parents may have to remind them that the baby has a special growing place, with its own separate access route, quite distinct from all parts of the digestive system.

The child who spoke of the daddy who "puts his hand in his tummy and gets the seed out," while "the mommy gets the egg out of her tummy," can be questioned:

PARENT: Can you put your hand inside your tummy?

CHILD: No.

PARENT: Then do you think the mommy and daddy can really put their hands in their tummies?

CHILD: I don't know exactly, 'cause he can't really open up all his tummies. I don't really know.

PARENT: There must be another way. Do you want to know how they get the sperm and the ovum together?

If the child says "No," a parent may reply, "Okay, you let me know when you want me to tell you more about it." If the child says "Yes," the parent might continue:

PARENT: The daddy's sperm are in his testicles and they come out through his penis. The mommy's vagina is a tunnel to where her ovum are. So if the daddy put his penis into her vagina, the sperm could go through the tunnel to the ovum.

The image of the vagina as a tunnel is an important one. We have seen that children can conclude that sexual intercourse "helps the baby come out," or that the sperm must "bite a hole" to get to the ovum. Unless children know that this passageway for sperm and baby exists before intercourse, they may adopt fearsome violent images of the penis forcefully penetrating the mother's body to create the opening. Gadpaille points out that members of both sexes sometimes have fantasies that their genitals, or the genitals of the other sex, may be mutilating, dangerous weapons. Clarity, simplicity, and thoroughness in describing anatomical differences can help prevent these damaging ideas.

It is also good to introduce the idea that sexual intercourse involves love and pleasure, going beyond the mechanics of reproduction to include sexuality and emotion. Children will not spontaneously believe that sexual intercourse is a pleasurable expression of intimacy and caring. But parents who convey that they enjoy and respect their own sexuality can counterbalance children's tendency to think about sex as aggression or, at best, a necessary medical maneuver that takes a lot of time and bother. If Mommy and Daddy are unashamed and say that sex feels good, the child will have a built-in reminder that, appearances and "dirty-talking" classmates to the contrary, it can't be all bad.

This is the part of sex education that most directly involves questions of value. Parents will likely have deeply felt convictions about when and with whom it is okay to be sexually intimate. One possible way of continuing the discussion is suggested here:

PARENT: When a man and a woman love each other, they want to be close to each other in many ways. They like to hug and kiss and touch each other all over. That's called making love. When a man and a woman make love, sometimes the man puts his penis into the woman's vagina. That feels very good to them. And that's how the sperm gets into the mommy's body to join with the ovum and make a baby. Sometimes people make love to make a baby, but most of the time they make love because they want to be close and loving and because it feels good.

6

The Reporters— Level Four

Most of the Level Four children I talked with were between seven and twelve. Although they may know the physical "facts of life," they don't understand why sperm and ovum must unite before new life can begin. Asked to explain the necessity of fertilization, many children simply describe sexual intercourse and assert flatly "that's just the way people have their babies" or "that's the way I learned it."

Called "Reporters" because of their concern for accuracy, they are reluctant to speculate on the rationale behind the facts they have adopted on the strength of the authority of parents, teachers, or books. Although aware that there are things they don't understand, they rigorously exclude theorizing without evidence. At no other level of reasoning were children so hesitant to guess when they did not feel certain.

When they do explain why male and female contributions are necessary to create a baby, the formation of the embryo resembles a concrete adding on of parts, rather than following a more organic pattern of growth. Because they usually believe that intercourse takes place for the sole purpose of making babies, they see all babies as planned and not wanting babies as sufficient for avoiding conception and birth.

They are still engrossed by the social relations of reproduction, attentive to the emotions prospective parents ought to feel for each other, and concerned with how families are started and maintained. Love and nurturance, as well as biological ties, make for parenthood. Love is no longer seen as sufficient to produce a child, but parents must love each other to have a child and must love the child to continue being parents.

By the time the child has reached Level Four, it seems to him as if the world is full of laws. Objects are subject to laws of motion and transformation. A ball of clay rolled into a sausage contains neither more nor less clay than the original ball. Earlier, children claimed that the sausage had more clay because it is longer. Now they see that, although longer, it is not as thick as the ball. They can keep track of the changes in both dimensions and conclude that the amount is the same. They are no longer deceived by an obvious change that temporarily overshadows other changes that balance it out. Perhaps more important, they can mentally reverse and retrace the operation. "If you roll the sausage back into a ball," they explain, "it will be the same as it was before. Since you didn't add any clay or take any away, it has to be the same amount of clay."

Recognizing the equality of two quantities, weights, numbers, or volumes, despite misleading changes in their appearance, is called *conservation*. Conservation is one of what Piaget calls the *concrete operations*. Operations are internalized actions that are coherent, systematic, and reversible. Concrete operations involve real objects that can be seen and touched.

Concrete operations require that we stop focusing only on a limited amount of the information available. Children capable of these mental actions can focus on several aspects of a situation at the same time. They are sensitive to transformations and can reverse the direction of their thinking. They can organize objects into classes and understand which classes are included in more general classes. For example, they can now tell you whether there are more roses or more flowers in a bunch of a dozen flowers, eight of them roses.

For the first time they can coordinate two relations that move in different directions to arrive at the accurate sequence. They can arrange a series of dolls according to height and then give each doll the appropriate size cane from a set of sticks differing in length. They can do this even if the sticks are presented in reverse order from the dolls. What they cannot do is solve a similar but verbal problem: If Joan is taller than Susan and shorter than Ellen, which girl is the tallest of the three? At this level, the child first thinks that Joan and Susan are tall, while Joan and Ellen are short. This line of reasoning leads to the conclusion that Susan is the tallest child, followed by Joan and then Ellen. This solution is the exact opposite of that produced by adult logic about relations.

Children's reasoning that is connected with their actual beliefs, grounded in the direct evidence of their senses, will be logical at this level. Comparisons, relations, inclusion, ordering and measurement of concrete objects are well within their ability.

What they cannot yet do is reason logically about ideas or hypothetical statements based on premises they don't believe. They cannot, for example, tell what is absurd about a sign which reads "Do not read this sign." Either they accept the statement and fail to see what is absurd or they reject the whole statement as silly and fail to grasp the formal absurdity in the situation. Not until eleven or twelve, and the development of what Piaget calls *formal operations,* do children become capable of making deductions about abstract concepts and systematizing their own beliefs. At Level Four, children's thinking is operational but still concrete.

Starting with Level Four, children give primarily physiological explanations of reproduction. They can think logically about objects and people and can consider past and future. They understand the idea of cause and effect. They know that identity lasts a lifetime.

Loath to speculate about things they don't know, children

at this level limit their explanations to the facts and nothing but the facts. When their knowledge is incomplete, they refuse to share their guesses or work the problem out further. Although they may know the physical "facts of life," they don't understand why sperm and egg must come together before new life can begin. "That's the way I learned it" or "that's just how people have their babies," they told me by way of explanation. Much of their knowledge is rote repetition of what they have been taught. And respectful of the authority of their sources of information—parents, teachers, and the almighty written word—they feel no need to probe further.

Many of the children at this level first responded to questions about how people get babies with disclaimers: "I don't know much about it," "Well, they just have them," or "I only know one thing." They were aware that there were gaps in their understanding, but, unlike their younger sisters and brothers, they were rigorous in excluding theories they could not back up with evidence.

Only little kids believe in magic. Now they laugh and scoff at their earlier belief in mythical creatures, the elves, gremlins, and Easter bunnies that can't be seen. But neither can they see sperm, ova, the special passageway in women through which the baby exits, or, in most cases in this culture, the mysterious sexual coupling. Trained that seeing is believing, it is no wonder that they are not confident that they can fully explain the invisible events that strain their understanding.

They do know that paternity is a matter of biology as well as social relationships. Most talked about the meeting of male and female cells during sexual contact, although the terms they used to describe the materials involved and the explicitness of their descriptions varied considerably. When parents "mate," "do it," or "make love," according to children who sometimes refuse to clarify what they mean, the "seeds" or "eggs" or "genes" get together and a baby begins.

Why does that have to happen for a baby to start developing? They don't really know and usually refuse to venture a guess.

Frank thought the sperm existed primarily to provide an escort service: "The sperm reaches the eggs. It looses 'em and brings 'em down to the forming place. I think that's right, and it grows until it's ready to take out."

What grows?

"The baby," he said, "the egg," indicating that the sperm didn't form part of the developing infant, growing in its special forming place.

Nine-year-old Frank was uncomfortable, at first, talking about sex. Very aware that many of the words he knew were not acceptable in polite conversation with adults, he kept checking with me about his choice of vocabulary. When I asked him how people get babies, he wavered: "They just get 'em. Well, I know, but I don't know how to put it in words . . . Well, the mother gets pregnant and gets the baby. How should I put it? Well, let's see. Well, then the male and the female mate. Is that a good word? And how shall I say this? Is it okay? Can I say sperm? The sperm reaches the eggs and then just bring them down to some place, loosen them and brings them to some special place."

The place is special, but its location is still a mystery. Other questions remain. "If the tubes are tied in the female, whatever that is, where the eggs are, then they can mate without having a child," Frank explained before going on to tell me that they would not, of course, mate if they didn't want a baby. But wanting a child is not enough. Chance plays a role in the progression of events, and mating does not always result in babies: "Maybe the sperms just doesn't reach the egg right."

Karen, who is eight, explained: "I don't know much about it. Well, I know one thing. The man and the woman get together. And then they put a speck, then the man has his seed and the woman has an egg. They have to come together or else the baby, the egg won't really get hatched very well. The seed makes the egg grow. It's like plants. If you plant a seed, a flower will grow."

Karen's return to the agricultural metaphor is a reminder that children's thought develops in a spiral, not a straight line. They circle back to the same issues, but deal with old information at a more sophisticated level.

She knew that sexual intercourse provides a means for the seed and egg to come together. She knew that both are necessary to create new life, but she had no clear idea of why this was so. Nor did she attempt to reason her way to a solution: "Well, see the man and the woman put the, see the man puts his penis into and the lady puts her vagina, and then the man puts his penis in the lady's vagina, and that's how the seed gets to touch the egg. The seed makes the egg grow, and then the egg grows fatter and fatter, and then the baby's inside the uterus. Then the woman who's having the baby gets fatter and fatter. Then after nine months the woman has a baby, and then you go to the hospital and the doctor takes it out."

I probed further, trying to find the rationale for the procedures she had outlined.

ME: Does the seed have to touch the egg for a baby to grow?

KAREN: No, if you want to adopt one that's easy to do.

ME: That's another way of getting a baby. But if a mommy and daddy wanted a baby to grow in the uterus, is that the only way to get it started?

KAREN: I don't know any other way.

ME: Can a baby grow inside the uterus if that doesn't happen?

KAREN: I don't think so.

ME: Every time they do that do they get a baby?

KAREN: Well, not if the woman takes birth-control pills, it doesn't happen.

ME: Why do they need the seed to touch the egg for a baby to grow?

KAREN: The egg won't hatch.

ME: Can you explain more about what you mean by that?

KAREN: 'Cause if the seed doesn't get to meet the egg then it will just break up and nothing will happen. The egg and the seed will just break up. It won't come together like it's supposed to do. The egg won't grow. It just gets split up, and it won't do anything.

ME: What is there about its coming together that makes the baby?

KAREN: I don't know.

ME: Can the egg grow into a baby without the seed?

KAREN: I don't think so.

ME: Can the seed grow into a baby without the egg?

KAREN: I don't know, but I don't think so.

Her facts are essentially accurate. It's unclear, when she talks about the baby or the egg "hatching," whether she thinks that the baby is already in the egg, fully formed and ready to grow if touched by the seed or prepared to disintegrate if things don't go according to schedule. But her image of the egg is still inseparably tied to those in cartons in the supermarket. The Provincial Museum on Vancouver Island has a drawing on the wall of its typical turn-of-the-century bedroom that might well picture Karen's concept of "hatching": It shows a baby crawling out of an eggshell.

According to Karen, babies grow "whenever you want to have a baby," and her mother doesn't have a baby growing in her uterus " 'cause she didn't do it." Even children who mention birth-control pills or tying tubes may still maintain that intercourse is only for making babies. Others, who can describe how sperm meets egg, may think that a couple's wishes can determine whether or not a baby will grow.

"Every time people make love," explained twelve-year-old Beth, "they don't always get a baby. 'Cause sometimes they don't want to have a baby. If they want to, they'll have a baby."

How does making love work to make a baby?

"Well, the seeds meet the other seeds, then they make a baby. The seeds from the mother meet the other seeds from the man. And then it forms a baby. Then the baby starts to grow in the mother's stomach, and it keeps growing and growing and growing, and then it comes out. By its head first, so it can breathe. It comes out when the mother's usually in labor. That means when they're in pain, I guess."

I asked her why the seeds have to meet the other seeds for the baby to start. "It just works," she said, "I don't know how."

"The man puts his penis into the lady's vagina," Wilma, who is nine, told me when I asked her how people get babies. "That's all I know." She didn't know what that had to do with getting babies, or so she said, but she doubted that babies could grow if that didn't happen. Nor did she think that a baby would grow every time, "because something goes wrong with the lady's body sometimes, I don't know what." I encouraged her to try to figure out how the babies start to form, but she wasn't interested in pursuing elusive memories. "I sort of learned something that it has to do with their genes in their body but then I forgot the rest," she told me. When I asked her what genes were, she said she had forgotten that, too, and couldn't or wouldn't guess.

Beverly, who is eight, began by telling me how much her sex education differed from her mother's: "My mother said that her mother told her, when she was real little that babies come down the chimney by storks. But she doesn't tell me that. She tells me something different. We have this baby book, and it's about how you were born, and all the ways that it's been done. But I haven't actually read the book, so I only know one thing. It comes out of the mother's uterus. I don't know how this works but first there's sort of like this crack in the uterus. And it takes about seven or eight months. And then the baby sort of starts pushing out. And usually there's a doctor with you there, to cut the cord so the baby isn't attached all the time to the mother."

I asked her how the baby starts to be in its mother's uterus.

"The father gives the rest of the egg to the mother. When the man sticks his penis into the vagina."

Why does he have to give the rest of the egg to the mother?

She explained: "Because the mother just has *half* of it. It's like a egg has two parts. It's just like—we had a big salami, which is whole, and we cut it in half, and we just go like that," she said, bringing her hands together in front of her. "I just thought of the word that happens when two eggs get together. I think it's called the sperm."

What's called the sperm?

"That's when the two eggs get together. The father has one part of the egg and the mother has the other part of the egg. And they have to get together to have a baby."

Again I asked why.

"Well, I think the mother has half of the body, and the father has half of the other body."

"Can you explain some more about that?" I persisted.

"Maybe I could," she said, "but I just can't think of it."

Her version of fertilization is reminiscent of the Alcibiades myth in Plato's *Symposium*. Before birth, according to this myth, we were each part of a joined pair of people. Our task in life is to find our other half in order to recreate the sense of wholeness we dimly remember and long to reexperience. So, for Beverly the male and female contributions must be concrete and tangible, half a body here and half a body there, like a salami. The fusion of two different cells to form one new entity that is not yet what it will become is too complex a concept to be understood at this level.

Nine-year-old Wanda began by talking about the kind of relationship a couple must have to become parents: "Well, first a man and a woman have to like each other and be with each other a lot. They have to sleep with each other sometimes, and then—do you want the whole everything for the exact stuff, I don't know everything about how it does and things—and then after a long time the woman starts getting a little bit big, starts getting big around here. Then in about six months she has a baby and the baby comes out of here." She pointed first to her abdomen and then to her crotch.

I asked her how the baby starts to grow.

WANDA: From a seed.

ME: Where does the seed come from?

WANDA: From the man and the woman. I think it goes through the man's penis. And it goes into the woman, I don't know where.

ME: Why do they need two seeds, one from the man and one from the woman?

WANDA: To make a boy or a girl. Because otherwise they can't start growing.

ME: How does it start growing?

WANDA: When they meet there's a lot of seeds from the woman going around. The one seed from the man goes and touches, gets one seed from the woman and then they stick together, and then they just start growing.

ME: Tell me more about the seed from the woman. Is it there all the time?

WANDA: It's just there at special times. And some women can't have babies.

ME: Why?

WANDA: When they're about over forty-five, I think then they can't, but I don't know. And some women just can't at any time, but I don't know why.

She has the numbers reversed, giving a lone male seed many female seeds to choose among, and implies that male and female must contribute seeds in order for there to be both girl and boy babies. Perhaps the mother's seed has special duties to perform in making girls, while seeds from the father play the more important part in the formation of boys. We cannot be sure, because she is not.

While children at this level may be unclear about why sperm and ovum must come together to form a new life, they have an intuitive understanding that both father and mother contribute toward making their children the people they will become. "Who would I be if my mommy had married another man?" they may wonder, knowing that they would not then be themselves. Yet they go on to ask themselves, "Who else could I possibly have been? Because I am me."

A woman I talked with remembered her childhood feeling that she was unwanted because her mother might have preferred another man to her father: "I had a really traumatic experience. I didn't really know until I was in fourth grade that my mother had been married before she was married to my father. And he was my real father, and my brother's real father, but I hadn't known that this other person had existed at all. And when I found out, I was just wiped out. Because I figured that she hadn't really wanted me. It wasn't a divorce. The man died. And I was convinced that she really didn't want me to exist and didn't want to be married to my father. She would have much preferred to be married to the other person. And then I wouldn't have been."

For younger children, mommies are "grown-up ladies" who simply "grew into mommies" regardless of whether they have children. Later, the relationship to children becomes the deciding factor in who is a mommy or daddy, defined as "people who like children" and take care of them. Now both biology and social relationships are taken into account. Children are now aware that the biological fact of birth is accompanied by a set of social expectations about parenting.

When I asked Karen how mothers get to be mothers, she said: "When they have a baby. It just makes that, if you have a baby, you just turn into a mother. It's a special name for the person to have. It's a special name that they call her, and that's how they call them."

"Why do you have this mother?" I asked. Her answer suggests a lottery, in which chance distributes babies among the population of possible mothers: "Because my mother, the people that had me are the only ones that wanted to have me right then, and so then it turned out to be me with them. And so that's why my mother got to be my mother. Seven and a half years ago. My father got to be my father the same way my mother got to be my mother, except he didn't go to the doctor and have me. There's only one person who has me, and that's my mother. But my father's the one who helped hatch me. 'Cause if my mother didn't have the seed, then the egg never would have grown."

Many of the children answered the questions about how people get to be parents by saying simply "when they get married and they have children." Marriage is an even more definitive criterion of parenthood for fathers than for mothers, since they often add that their mothers are "the one that borned me." Fathers get to be fathers when the woman they are married to has a baby. Pressed to explain further, they may add, as did Wanda, "My father got a seed and gave it to my mother, and my mother had a child and that's me, and so he's my father." She was aware that there are other ways as well. When I asked her if that was the way all fathers get to be parents, she replied: "No, not always. They can adopt a baby. Or if they live with a woman, and the woman has a baby, even though he didn't have it, and the woman dies or gives the baby to the man." So love and care, as well as biological ties, can make a person a parent.

Like Beverly, children at this level were more likely than before to form categories to describe parents as "a person who takes care of you," although the group defined by this definition is too inclusive to be accurate. Beverly was also a little confused about the complexities of some family relationships. "They grow up. Then they have to get married, and then they have to have a baby," she said, explaining how mothers get to be mothers. She has the mother she does by virtue of the relationship between her parents. Because she knows from the experience of her friends' parents that marriages do end, she is not sure that parenting relationships do not end with them:

"I have this mother, 'cause my mother liked my father and my father liked my mother. Or else, if my mother and father got divorced I would have had a different mother." "You would?" I asked. "Yes. Well, that would depend on who would, you know, like if my father, he would have to get a new wife. But if my mother took me, she would have to go get a new husband. It would really depend on who would take me."

"Wouldn't your mother always be your mother, even if you didn't live with her?" I asked.

"I guess so," she replied, not entirely convinced. When I asked her how her father got to be her father, she concentrated on the feelings her parents had for each other: "Well, he wouldn't have been my father if, actually if he didn't like my mother, he wouldn't have been my father. If he liked another woman."

"Well, one thing is that he liked your mother. But maybe lots of people liked your mother? Why is he your father?" I asked.

"Once my mother almost married a different guy. And also he used to live in Boston, and my father once liked another woman. But he got to be my father because he just liked my mother better than the other one."

"Did he do anything besides like your mother to get to be your father?"

"I guess they married each other. Well, actually if you want a baby you have to be married. 'Cause the father has one part of the egg, and the mother has the other part of the egg. And they have to get together to have a baby."

So, for her, a loving relationship between the parents was the first prerequisite for having a baby. Then marriage brings the two half eggs together to make one whole baby.

Talking with Level Three Children

Knowing that they will soon be Reporters, we can help clean up some confusions for the In-Betweens, the children at Level Three. Level Three children already restrict themselves to explanations of reproductive processes that are technically possible. They are busy evaluating many of their former beliefs, reconsidering how lingering ideas from early childhood measure up to their new experience of reality, and rejecting the artificialism and animism of their more obviously precausal theories. Parents now can help clear up misapprehensions, explain why some of their children's beliefs are mistaken, and provide new physiological explanations. Children moving toward Level Four thinking are eager for facts.

Ellen, who believed that the sperm "bites a hole with its little mouth and swims into the vagina," can be led to understand that the sperm does not need to inflict injury on either penis or vagina to arrive at its destination. Like most children her age, she has probably discarded the idea that inanimate objects move of their own free will, acting purposefully as do people; doors, stones, and toys are no longer mistaken for deliberate friends or foes. But mercury, the sun, and other things that move independently may continue to be seen as animate. Sperm, which look like tadpoles and locomote like minnows, are especially difficult to distinguish from complete organisms.

PARENT: I know sperm look like tadpoles. And the way they move *does* look like swimming. But a sperm is not a whole animal. Unlike a fish, it has no mouth to bite with. It can't decide where to go. It just has to move with the semen until it gets near the ovum.

CHILD: Isn't it alive?

PARENT: It is alive, because it's a part of a living creature. Our whole bodies are alive—skin, bones, eyes, stomach —everything is made of living cells, tiny bits of living matter. But while all the stuff of which we're made is alive, none of the little bits can think, or move, or behave as a person or an animal can.

CHILD: Well, then how does it get out of the daddy and into the mommy?

PARENT: There's a tube in the daddy's penis so the sperm can go from the testicles, where they're made, out of his body at the tip of his penis. When the mommy and daddy are making love, the muscles around his penis pump semen out through his penis into the mommy's vagina. That's called "ejaculating the semen." Her vagina is like a tunnel, and there's already a hole there so the penis can fit in without having to make a new opening.

CHILD: It sounds yukky.

PARENT: I know. A lot of children think so. It's hard to imagine how good it can feel until you're more grown up. You know how nice it feels when you touch your penis [clitoris and vulva]? Well, that can give you some idea why people like to make love. Sometimes a special feeling called "orgasm" happens, when they feel very excited and after that they feel very relaxed. Both men and women have these special feelings of orgasm, and orgasm is usually the time when men ejaculate.

This is also a good time to help children sort out how feelings and social arrangements for childbearing relate to the physiology of reproduction. Clarity about their parents' values is as important to them as correcting inaccuracies in their ideas.

Values play a vital role in human sexuality. How and with whom to relate sexually is a subject about which everyone seems to have strong feelings. Most parents want to teach their children that sexual feelings are a natural part of human relating, rather than taboo, shameful, dangerous, and requiring either avoidance or repression. At the same time, they would like their children to reserve full sexual expression for a very special relationship, so that it is neither trivialized nor divorced from emotional intimacy.

In talking with children about values, it is important to distinguish among deeply felt principles, social conventions, and physiological processes. While parents may want to teach their children not to engage in sexual intercourse until they feel love for and are loved by, or married to, a partner, no parent who wants to adequately prepare children for eventual sexual maturity will lead them to believe that conception is impossible without either love or marriage.

Frank described conception in the following manner: "I guess it's like mothers and fathers are related, and their loving each other forms a baby. I don't know how it really comes, just by loving and stuff. I guess the love forms the beans, and I guess the beans hatches the egg."

His parents have obviously communicated to him their belief that it is critical that parents have a loving, deep commitment to each other before deciding to have a baby. He has already assimilated this integral part of their value system, and they would probably want to begin by validating that part of his explanation:

PARENT: It's really important for a baby that its mother and father love each other and love the baby, so that when the baby is born they can take good care of it. But loving is a feeling and can't start the baby all by itself. A baby is a living creature, and it starts growing from living material. When the mother and father make love, a sperm from the father goes through his penis into the mother's vagina. When the sperm joins with an ovum in the mother, the sperm and the ovum form one new thing, which grows into a baby.

This concept that the sperm and the ovum, once joined, create a new entity that develops into a baby is one that can be introduced to children who talk about each parent contributing "half a body," although it will take some time for them to assimilate this very complex idea.

Marriage, like love, should be differentiated from biological necessity in talking about reproduction. Children can be taught that this valuable social arrangement is important for the baby's welfare without being persuaded that avoiding the wedding ceremony is an effective contraceptive. A parent might say:

PARENT: I believe that it's very important that people are married before they have a baby [or before they have sexual intercourse]. But it isn't the wedding that gives you the seed. Babies are started when the sperm and the ovum get together during sexual intercourse. People can start a baby without being married, or even without wanting to start a baby. The sperm and the ovum don't know or care whether the people want the baby or can make a good home for the baby. When a sperm and an ovum join, a baby starts to grow. So people have to make sure that they don't let the sperm and the ovum get together until they are ready to take good care of a baby.

This can lead to a discussion both of contraception and the parents' values about when and with whom sexual intercourse should occur. It is wise to include the fact that other people may feel differently about standards of sexual behavior, and why you disagree with them. The world abounds with examples of different styles of dealing with sexuality, and it is helpful to children to know where their parents stand and why.

For many children lingering over the remnants of the myth of manufacture, it is the doctor who assumes responsibility for all the elusive, mysterious aspects of making babies. He tells the mother she is going to have a baby and takes it out, and, according to some children, without his intervention the baby might never have begun at all. Some children believe it is the doctor who puts the seed in the mother's vagina; others think he makes the seed from chemicals from his medicine cabinet or that the medicine itself starts the baby. While doctors deserve credit when it is due, this mystification of their importance fosters the illusion that they are omniscient, omnipotent agents of human destiny rather than skilled but fallible health workers whose judgment can be open to question. A parent might say:

PARENT: Doctors are very helpful to mothers who are having babies. They can check to see if the baby is growing the way it should and that the mother is taking special care of herself to keep healthy when she is pregnant. They also are very helpful in getting the baby out, especially if there is something unusual happening, like the baby being turned around inside the mother. But people had babies for a long time even before there were doctors. Most of the time, other women came to help the mother when the time came for the baby to come out. Mostly they helped keep things clean and kept the mother company, telling her what had helped them when they had babies.

7

The Theoreticians— Level Five

Children at Level Five are now willing to speculate about why sperm and ovum must unite to form new life. Going beyond rote repetition of the facts they have been taught, they arrive at theories that echo the history of scientific thinking about embryology. Not quite able to come up with an explanation of how two things can become one qualitatively different entity, they give either sperm or ovum credit for containing a miniature embryo; the other is relegated to a supporting role. Either the baby is said to be *really* in the ovum, needing the sperm only to catalyze its growth or give it energy, or, alternatively, it is the sperm that turns into a baby, given the nourishment and hospitable environment of the ovum. All see parenthood as a biological and a social relationship, but most seem to assume that the physiological aspects of reproduction have more explanatory value than the social. Children may begin to give Level Five explanations between ten and thirteen. It is difficult to set an upper age limit to this group, since many adults' thought about conception would be classified at Level Four.

Why am I living?
Why was I born?
Who am I?
Where did I come from?

The intense preoccupation of humankind with the meaning of existence has echoed these questions through the ages. As a species capable of reflecting on our own experience, human beings are denied the unquestioning acceptance of life, birth, and death that marks our brother and sister creatures. Other animals are born, mature, mate, give birth, and die with far greater equanimity than we can muster. Instead, we wonder, question, muse, brood, speculate, and investigate the whys and wherefores of our lives. The more choice we perceive, the greater our need for reason to lead us down the most propitious path. When our actions seem inevitable or unrewarding, we seek some greater purpose than they may be seen to serve.

Prospecting in the hills of life's beginnings and endings, humanity often found the gold of meaning. Mysteries that transcended our ability to see, hear, taste, touch, or smell their secrets, birth and death seemed to promise an answer to the eternal question of the meaning of existence, for birth and death define life by setting its limits.

We saw in Chapter 4 that children's first theories about the world are based on their knowledge of their own bodies, behavior, and thoughts. They personify the sun, the moon, and the wind, attributing human intentions and actions to the world of nature. In this respect, children recapitulate the history of our species. Peoples who preceded us in time also explained the world in animistic terms: the wind as the breath of unseen gods, thunder as the wrath and vengeance of a great spirit, rain or fair weather as gifts from heavenly protectors. Other peoples saw the world as manufactured by an omniscient and omnipotent God, who designed the valleys and mountains, seas and deserts, birds and beasts, all according to plan. Scientific inquiry has revealed, without necessarily challenging the existence of a higher spiritual force in the universe, that the formation of the natural world was not the work of a giant sculptor. Instead, the creation of the world was a gradual unfolding of physical processes, encompassing a multitude of changes, following natural laws intrinsic to the elements of matter.

The development of children's thinking about many subjects parallels the history of people's beliefs through the ages. Reproduction is no exception. Like young children first discovering how people get babies, earlier peoples first were limited in their knowledge to the fact that babies grow in their mothers' bodies. They, too, wondered where they were before birth, and spun theories of preexistence in other places or previous incarnations. They, too, often believed that the function of sexual intercourse was to open a passageway so that the baby might first enter and then be liberated from its cradle of flesh. Conception remained the great mystery, taking place in head or breast as well as womb, and often depending on the participation of spirits, sun, or rain. There are people alive today who do not yet know about biological paternity.

It was not until 1875 that Oscar Hertwig first discovered that the ovum and sperm each had a nucleus and that the two cells could unite and become one. Two years later, Edouard van Beneden found that the contents of these nuclei were basically similar and that the new cell formed by their fusion then begins to divide into two, four, many cells. In 1879, Walter Fleming witnessed the chromosomes dividing, so that genetic information from each parent could be traced to each cell of the developing child.

Until the 1870s, then, scientists and philosophers throughout history had speculated erroneously about the origin of babies. It was not only people we might label "primitive" who made these errors about the material ingredients that formed the new life, but the wisest and most learned men of science. In pursuing the answers to these age-old questions about the origin of babies, children seem to share many of the beliefs that long characterized the search for an understanding of human beginnings.

A complete summary of the history of embryology would

be inappropriate here. What is important for us to explore briefly are two of the leading theories held by investigators for many years, because Level Five Theoreticians subscribe to one or the other theory of procreation.

Level Five children believe that the baby is preformed in either sperm or ovum. The embryo is complete unto itself, they believe, and sexual intercourse merely provides the conditions necessary for it to develop. In the history of embryology, *preformation* is used to refer to growth without differentiation. This means that all living creatures were thought to preexist in miniature in the seeds of their parent plants and animals. Preformation theories include Ovism, whereby the embryo is thought to preexist in the ovum, and Animalculism, which claims that the embryo is fully contained in the sperm.

Aristotle expounded at length on Ovist theory. He believed that the material basis for the embryo was provided by the female, while the spiritual component was supplied by the male. According to Aristotle, the semen supplied "form" to the embryo and whatever the female produced supplied the matter fit for shaping; her clay was molded into human form by the sculpting action of the man's semen. His leading hypothesis was that the matter shaped in this way was menstrual blood. Aristotle's theory of conception was based on his belief that the male embodies effectiveness and activity, while the female represents natural existence and passivity, so that her contribution must be material and inert. This theory was elaborated in early Roman times by Pliny, who described how it worked: "The seed of the male, acting as sort of a leaven, causes the menstrual blood to unite and assume a form, and in due time it acquires life and assumes a bodily shape." Sexual intercourse gave "life" to materials already within the female, catalyzing their growth. The father was the provider of spiritual rather than material contributions to his offspring.

From the death of Aristotle, in the fourth century B.C.,

there is little recorded history in the science of embryology until the sixteenth century. Post-Aristotelian Ovists held that all embryos were produced from smaller embryos in the unfertilized eggs. The ovary of an ancestress was said to contain, in miniature, all of her descendants. Before the egg cell was discovered accidentally by Karl Ernst von Baer in the early nineteenth century, Ovists for the past three centuries had thought of the ovum as an oval-shaped body in the uterus. Indeed, ten years after von Baer's discovery a distinguished scientific society awarded a prize for a paper that put forth the belief that the ovum in mammals is first created in the fluid effused from the uterus after intercourse. According to Ovists of that time, the "ovum" merely needed to be "bathed in the spermatic liquor," which would then act upon a preformed embryo in the "ovum." Von Baer himself believed that sexual intercourse served to free the ovum from the ovary. To him the ovum was languid and quiescent, requiring the more rompish, energetic sperm to give it life.

Several of the children I interviewed might also be called Ovists. These children seemed to describe the sperm as a catalyst, energizing or giving life to the embryo latent in the egg. Twelve-year-old William was one of them. Asked how people get babies, he replied: "Well, they have intercourse, and then the sperm fertilizes the egg. And then it starts to develop and turns into an embryo. And it starts to grow, and when it's ready, it just comes out."

When asked what fertilization is and how it works to start a baby, he told me: " 'Fertilize' means when the sperm enters the egg. I guess it gives life to it or energy. I guess the egg just has sort of an undeveloped embryo, and when the sperm enters it, it makes it come to life. It gives it energy and things like that."

William had a more detailed, technically accurate concept of other aspects of human reproduction: "Intercourse is when the male inserts his penis into the lady's vagina. And then he has an orgasm, and then that makes the sperm come out.

And then that enters into the lady's uterus, and if she has an egg coming down the Fallopian tubes, the sperm fertilizes it and 'comes an embryo."

How the egg " 'comes an embryo" is the most complex part of a process that he otherwise understands quite well. He described pregnancy as "when you stop the menstrual cycle and the embryo starts growing, and it turns into a fetus, and keeps just getting bigger." He knew that intercourse did not always eventuate in pregnancy, "because not all the time the lady has an egg in her Fallopian tubes, and when it reaches the uterus and it's not fertilized it just dissolves."

For eleven-year-old Kent, the task of the sperm is to "hatch the egg, so the baby can come out." He guessed that if this were to not occur, "the baby doesn't start to grow, it just stays like this big." He held his hands about four inches apart. "The sperms make the baby grow."

"Well, they intercourse," he told me in response to my question about how people get babies. "Then the sperm goes to the ovary and it hatches, and the baby grows. Intercourse gets the sperm to the ovary to hatch the egg." He knew that intercourse did not always lead to a new baby: "Well, sometimes it doesn't work. Sometimes you could take pills. And sometimes it just doesn't work, like the sperms don't get all the way through to the ovary."

Kent was one of the few children at this level to comment on the difficulty of talking about sexual matters. "I don't know why it's hard to talk about. I guess it's 'cause it's obscene language. Even though I use it all the time." But talking with the boys in the neighborhood was different from talking with me. "It's because you're a grown-up," he told me, explaining the omissions in his description of procreation and his sporadic laughter. "I don't tell my mother what intercourse means either." "Is it because I'm a grown-up or because I'm a woman?" I pursued the question. " 'Cause you're a grown-up. I don't tell my father either."

Like Kent, Kevin was not too clear about how fertilization actually works, but he thought of it as the quickening of a previously static entity: "I don't really quite know what makes it able to work. I guess it just starts it off. I guess it just starts getting a heartbeat or something. I guess it just keeps developing after that." "It" must have already been in existence to get a heartbeat.

Karl's ideas are reminiscent of the Level Three child's shopping list of parts to be collected from mother and father. The hint of concrete assembly of parts is there, but the father's contribution follows Aristotle's thinking about what males have to give to their offspring.

"You said the baby won't grow if the sperm doesn't reach the egg. Why does that have to happen for a baby to grow?" I asked.

"Because the sperm have certain reflexes or something like that that would have to develop in the baby to be born."

"Then what is the egg for?"

"Well, I don't really know for sure, like they could have certain things that have the limbs, or your muscles or something like that. Whatever else the sperm doesn't have."

Later in the interview we returned to the same subject. "Can a baby grow if the egg and the sperm don't meet?"

"No," he expanded on his previous answer, "because the sperm has things like maybe parts of the brain or certain cells that are needed to have a baby or something."

Knowing that both egg and sperm are needed to begin a new life, confused about why this is so and what each might have to offer, he assigned "reflexes" and "parts of the brain" to the sperm. These parts of the nervous system, from which thoughts and dreams emanate and behavior takes its direction, are the material embodiment of the spirituality or life force that the Ovist tradition assigns to the male.

Twelve-year-old Ellen included a more extensive definition of fertilization in telling me how people get babies: "Well, they have sexual intercourse. Then the man, he puts his penis in the lady's vagina and sperm comes out, and they go, if the lady's had her period and if her egg is in her ovary, a sperm will go into her egg, and it will fertilize it, and that becomes a baby. 'Fertilize' means it gives it kind of like . . . if a plant didn't have soil or anything, like something it could eat sort of, in a way, it wouldn't really be able to grow. I think that would be the same as with an egg. So 'fertilize' means kind of give it food and things like that."

The idea that the sperm provides nourishment for the egg was unusual, a turnabout of the more common explanation of preformation in the sperm. Perhaps the agricultural metaphor and the list of nutriments on the bottles of plant fertilizer had led to this impression. She was aware that there was some confusion in her story.

"How is it that the baby starts growing when the sperm goes into the egg?" I asked.

"I don't know," she replied. "I guess when it gets in there it just does something to the egg, and it makes it start growing. In some way. I never, in school or anything, they never really explained that in full detail."

"Can the egg grow if no sperm goes in it?"

"I don't think so."

"Can the sperm grow with no egg?"

Her answer epitomized the Ovist solution: "No, that doesn't have the baby. It's the egg that would have the baby in it."

The other side of the preformation coin is Animalculism. In contrast to Ovism, this difficult-to-pronounce theory was based on the ancient belief that genetic parenthood was exclusively a paternal matter. The biblical emphasis on the male seed and the patriarchal line of succession is well known. There is nary a female name in the sequence of "begats" that takes biblical history from the Flood to the story of Abraham. To read Genesis, in which Mizraim begat Ludim . . . Canaan begat Sidon . . . Joktan begat Almodad . . . Shem begat Elam . . . and Arphaxad begat Salah, you might think that women had nothing to do with bringing into being each new generation.

In the late seventeenth century, Anton van Leeuwenhoek discovered what he called "spermatic animalcules" by examining semen under a microscope. To many scientists of the two centuries that followed, this seemed prima facie evidence that a new baby has its origin in its father's sperm. Leeuwenhoek believed that the ovum served only as food for the sperm, which entered it to grow into a new individual. Unaware of genetic dominance, he was further misled by mating tame white female rabbits with wild gray males. When all the offspring were gray, he took that as proof that the baby bunnies, despite being ushered into the world by their mamas, really came from Papa Rabbit. The common observation that conception does not occur without sexual intercourse and microscopic inspection of the active movements of the sperm were used as further evidence that the living material for the embryo was furnished exclusively by the father. The disproportion between the head and the body of the unborn or newborn child was also seen as proof that it derived from a sperm, which, they observed, also had a head that seemed to dwarf its tail.

"How do people get babies?" I asked Ollie, who is ten.

"Intercourse," he said.

"What does intercourse have to do with making a baby?"

"Well, the man has a sperm in him that's real tiny and has to go into the lady."

"And then what happens to the sperm?"

"It grows into a baby."

It is the sperm that grows into a baby. Ollie made no mention of any material contribution by the mother, who merely incubates the baby. "When the lady has the sperm, the whatever-it-is, the little baby, can just start growing." But the mother must be a careful and considerate incubator. According to Ollie, each instance of intercourse does not lead to a baby, and "If you eat too much, or walk around too much, or if you don't stay down in bed, just stay rested, it will die." It takes considerable effort to provide a hospitable environment for the apparently fragile sperm-child.

In this reproductive scheme, sexual intercourse is necessary in order to transfer the sperm from its point of origin in the father to an environment more conducive to its development in the mother. Twelve-year-old Tessa explained: "I think like the sperm is part of the baby. It goes inside the egg, and maybe the egg is food. Like in chickens, chickens have food. The sperm is something that grows if it gets the right atmosphere or something."

Her description of fertilization gives us a clue as to how her ideas were formed: "The man and the woman have sexual intercourse. The man's sperm goes into the woman's egg and starts a baby. Lots of sperm go and only one gets through, and the egg gets fertilized. 'Fertilized' means— like chickens have lots of eggs, and they don't let them get fertilized because if the chicken's egg got fertilized, then it would turn into a baby chick. Instead of just a yolk."

Her knowledge about chickens and her experience of eating their eggs helped to confuse her about people and their eggs. If chicken eggs, left unfertilized, become food, then perhaps the human egg, too, becomes food. If an egg without a sperm does not become a new being, then perhaps it is the sperm itself that grows to be a person when the time and place are suitable.

Eleven-year-old Kathy was more explicit about who does what in becoming parents. When I asked her how fathers get to be fathers, she told me that paternity is predominant in determining who their children are to be: "Well, if they're the man who made love to your mother, then they're your father because you really originally came out of him. And then went into your mother. And your mother, you were born to your mother, but you still have your father. You were a sperm inside of him there. He has millions of sperms, and when he let sperm into your mother, only one of them gets, usually, gets into the egg. And then that one is the one that gets grown up, and then grows, and then gets born. So that you're really his daughter or son. 'Cause he was the one that really had you first."

Kathy explained that the sperm dies if an egg has not been released, "so that sometimes they have to make love several times for the sperm to be able to come into the egg." When asked why the egg must be there for the sperm to develop into a baby, she replied: " 'Cause otherwise the sperm will have nothing to nourish it, or sort of keep it warm or, you know, able to move or something. It just has to have the egg to be able to do something—develop. It just dies if it doesn't have the egg." So the egg is assigned the cultural role usually allocated to women: to provide warmth and nourishment for the developing fetus. Like mother, like egg.

Robert, at twelve, gave a similar description. When asked what parents' "going to bed" has to do with getting babies, he answered: "Well, that's how the . . . well, the lady has an egg, and the man has a sperm. And they, sort of he fertilizes the egg, and then the egg slowly grows, the sperm grows into a baby inside the egg, and slowly develops, and in nine months it comes out of the lady."

"What does 'fertilize' mean?" I asked.

"Well, it means it gets inside the egg, the sperm does, it just sort of goes in. The egg before the sperm goes in is sort of like . . . well, I guess it doesn't have anything in it to grow. It just has food, and I guess a shell on the outside, or maybe some plastic coating like a membrane."

"Why does that have to happen for the baby to begin to grow?"

"Well, it's sort of the beginning, the beginning of the baby. It has to happen, because otherwise the sperm would just die, because it has no shelter on the outside to keep it alive, no food, nothing. And then the egg, there's nothing in it to grow, I guess. It has no . . . no . . . no living animal in there. It just has food and the outside. And he has to put the little thing in there, the man does, and then it starts to grow. And it just couldn't grow unless that little animal got inside the egg." So the sperm is a little animal that grows into a bigger animal with the proper care and feeding from the egg.

This quite explicit Animalculist theory of birth, like the Ovist and Animalculist explanations we looked at earlier, echoes scientists' earlier search for the facts of conception.

In trying to make sense to themselves in thinking about reproduction, children unknowingly follow the steps of other explorers after scientific truth. Surprisingly, the gender of the children did not seem to influence the theory they adopted, despite the precedence given to one sex or the other by the two theoretical camps. As many girls as boys saw the father as the parent of origin, with the mother providing food and shelter for the baby's growth. And as many boys as girls thought that the baby was *really* in the egg, with the sperm simply providing the reminder, jolt, or kick in the pants it needed to start growing.

"Well, number one," Robert had told me in beginning his explanation of procreation quoted above, "they probably get married, and they must like each other a lot." Children at this level have begun to see marriage as a social convention that most people follow before having children, rather than as a biological prerequisite for parenthood. A mother gets to be a mother by bearing children. Some consider that she starts to be a mother "when the egg was fertilized in her." Fathers get to be fathers by "sending the sperm in to her," or "when the woman has a baby, like his wife or something." Ellen emphasized that paternity was a social role as well as a biological relationship by stating that fathers get to be fathers "by being married to somebody or living with somebody who has a child."

Even though they now know that sexual contact can lead to pregnancy, with or without marriage, they still find it confusing to think about different family arrangements from the ones with which they are familiar. Teri told me that mothers get to be mothers "by marrying and having children." I asked her to elaborate on the connection between the two. "Well, you don't have to be married to have a baby," she replied, "but, um, if . . . I don't know if you can really be a family without being married, or just if you're a family with being married." Although assigning more weight to the physical determinants of reproduction, she was unsure of how to reconcile lessons about marriage as both socially important and physiologically extraneous in child-bearing. Successful integration of the various factors important in explaining conception and birth seems to require the more sophisticated reasoning of Level Six.

Talking with Level Four Children

Up to this point, we have been using the metaphors and thinking style of each level as a basis for talking intelligibly with children who are approaching that level from the level that precedes it. To do so now would be to lead them astray, reinforcing misconceptions rather than helping them to unravel the knots in their thinking.

Instead of talking with Level Four children in the pre-formist language of Level Five, parents can take advantage of their hunger for concrete information by presenting facts to fill some of the gaps in their knowledge of reproduction. For most children, many processes remain elusive; others may worry about half-digested lessons that irritate their sensitivities as they identify with either parent or fetus. While they both want and need more facts, they are also more aware of their parents' (and society's) attitudes about sexual matters, and may need some reassurance before they can ask questions freely. Embarrassment may persist, for even the most relaxed parents cannot eradicate the influence of the larger cultural milieu, but giggles need not be a barrier to understanding.

Regardless of their level of thinking, girls and boys need to learn about menstruation and seminal emissions *before* they reach the age at which these may actually happen to *them*. With the average age of the onset of menstruation, or menarche, steadily declining in Western industrialized coun-tries over the last century, most girls in this country have their first menstrual period when they are between eleven and fourteen years of age, but many begin earlier. For boys, nocturnal emissions, or "wet dreams," typically begin when they are about thirteen or fourteen, but, again, ages vary.

While children need to know about all the bodily changes that will accompany maturation, menstruation and nocturnal emissions are the most abrupt of these changes. Unlike growing taller, changing shape or voice, which may be noticed and commented on as they take place in your own children or their playmates, these less-visible events may occur unheralded. Unless boys know that "wet dreams" are a normal part of growing up, they may worry that they have wet the bed and feel embarrassed about appearing babyish.

PARENT: When boys mature, their testes begin to make sperm and their prostate begins to make semen. Semen is a thick, whitish fluid in which the sperm are carried out of the penis. When a man or boy is sexually excited, blood rushes to his penis, so that it gets harder and more sensitive and stands up "erect," which is why that is called "having an erection." If he continues to feel more excited, if he rubs his penis, semen spurts out of his penis. This is called "ejaculation," and he will feel an extra-special pleasure that leaves him feeling relaxed and good all over. This is called "orgasm." Ejaculation or orgasm can happen when he is masturbating or during sexual intercourse or even when he is dreaming about sex. If a boy or man ejaculates when he is sleeping, we call that a "wet dream" or "nocturnal emission," because "nocturnal" means "nighttime" and "emission" means "discharge" or "release." Men usually ejaculate at the same time as they have an orgasm, while women have the special pleasure of an orgasm without ejaculating.

At the first sign of menstrual blood, uninformed girls may worry that they have hurt themselves. They also need to be prepared about what to do if their first menstrual period begins while they are away from home.

A mother can introduce the subject of menstruation by

drawing attention to her purchase of tampons or sanitary napkins. Or a child may ask about these objects seen at home, or repeat stories relayed from other children. In explaining menstruation, diagrams of the female reproductive system can be very useful in showing children the parts of the body involved. After reviewing the reproductive organs, a parent might say:

PARENT: Every month, one ovum becomes ripe. This ovum leaves the ovary and travels down the Fallopian tube to the uterus. It travels very slowly. It takes five or six days to travel through the tube, which is only about four inchs long. The Fallopian tube is lined with fine, waving cells like hairs that push the ovum through to the uterus. While this is happening, the uterus is getting ready for the ovum to arrive. Do you know how it gets ready?

CHILD: It bleeds blood.

PARENT: In a way. The lining of the uterus gets thick and soft and spongy, because the mother's body directs more blood to the uterus to help form a nesting place in case a baby is started. If a sperm joins with the ovum, they attach to the soft, thick, spongy lining of the uterus, and grow into the beginnings of a baby, called an "embryo."

CHILD: What's an embryo?

PARENT: That's the name we call the developing baby when it just begins to grow in the uterus. But every ovum doesn't get to form part of an embryo. The ovum is only ripe for a couple of days. If no sperm unites with it, the ovum disintegrates. When this happens, there is no longer a need for the soft lining and the extra blood supply, because no baby is going to be kept comfortable and nourished. So the extra blood and lining pass through the vagina, and the woman wears a tampon or sanitary napkin to absorb the blood. It's not the same as bleeding when you fall and scrape your knee or when you cut yourself. The blood comes out pretty slowly, and it's extra blood, not the blood that circulates through her body. That's called "menstruation." And it happens about once a month, every time an ovum leaves an ovary and there is no sperm to unite with it while it's ripe.

I think it is better to speak of the unfertilized ovum, and the also-ran among the sperm in the race to fertilize the ovum, as disintegrating rather than dying. Because children may still mistake either sperm or ovum for a complete new life, saying that either "dies" can elicit funereal images of microscopic moribund babies.

We cannot cover all the questions that may arise for children trying to rethink prior misconceptions and remedy earlier omissions about sex and birth. Some of the more common questions, along with a short reply, follow.

Sexual Intercourse

CHILD: Janie says the man pees inside the lady to start a baby.

PARENT: What do you think?

CHILD: I don't think pee can help make a baby. But if he puts his penis in her vagina, the pee will go into her.

PARENT: I can see how you might think that. You're right that pee can't help make a baby. Urine is a waste product. It's part of what's left over after our bodies use up all of the nourishing parts of the food we eat and drink. Can you think of something else the man might be putting into the woman's vagina when they make love?

CHILD: Well, he needs to put in sperms, 'cause you need one sperm and one ovum to make a baby. But maybe sometimes he makes a mistake and pees instead.

PARENT: He can't make a mistake. Our bodies are made so that those kinds of mistakes don't happen. The penis only lets one kind of liquid through at a time. If semen is passing through the penis, no urine can get in. When a man is having sexual intercourse, only semen can pass through his penis.

CHILD: Good. I didn't want what Janie said to be true. It sounds awful.

PARENT: Do you have any other questions about sexual intercourse?

CHILD: Well, actually I wonder sometimes . . . grown-ups say they like doing that, but vaginas look real little and penises look too big to fit in. It sounds like it could hurt.

PARENT: Do you remember how the baby gets out of the mother's uterus?

CHILD: Yes, through her vagina. But you said the vagina is just a small opening. I don't see how the baby fits either.

PARENT: Most of the time the vagina is a narrow passageway from the uterus to the vulva. But the vagina can stretch large enough for a baby to be pushed through it. After the baby is born it goes back to its usual size.

CHILD: Well, I guess if the vagina can stretch to fit a baby, it can stretch to fit a penis.

PARENT: A baby is much bigger than a penis, so the vagina that can make room for a baby can certainly make room for a penis. Our bodies are wonderfully made to be able to do all the things that people need to do to live and reproduce.

Conception

CHILD: Aunt Ellen and Uncle Mike say they want to have a baby. Why don't they just have one?

PARENT: Not all grown-ups can have a baby as soon as they decide they want one. Sometimes they have to wait a long time for a baby to start to grow.

CHILD: But you told me the woman's body makes a new ovum every month.

PARENT: What else is needed to start a baby?

CHILD: A sperm. But lots and lots of sperm go into the woman when they sexual intercourse.

PARENT: Timing is real important. Both the ovum and the sperm have to be in the Fallopian tube and ripe at the same time. The woman doesn't usually know the exact time that the ovum becomes ripe, and it stays ripe for only forty-eight hours. And even though millions of sperm are ejaculated during sexual intercourse, not all of the sperm are able to get as far as the Fallopian tubes. And sperm only stay active for two to four days. After that, no sperm are available to join with the ovum. So it sometimes takes a long time before the parents can get an active sperm to a ripe ovum, which is the only way a baby can begin to grow.

Pregnancy

CHILD: How does the baby eat when it's in the uterus?

PARENT: How do you think?

CHILD: Well, I don't think it can eat cereal or bananas or milk with its mouth, like little babies do after they're born. If it opened its mouth, it would just swallow that stuff it floats in. But the baby needs the water to keep it from getting hurt if the mother falls or something.

PARENT: That's right. The sac of fluid helps keep the baby comfortable. It always stays the same temperature, no matter what the weather is outside, and it protects the baby by acting like a shock absorber. So how else do you think the baby can get the nourishment and the oxygen it needs?

CHILD: Maybe through that cord that goes to your belly button?

PARENT: Yes, the umbilical cord brings nourishment and oxygen from the bloodstream of the mother to the bloodstream of the baby. That's why the mother has to make sure she eats a lot of good, nourishing food when she's pregnant. She digests the food, and the things the baby needs to grow pass from her blood to the placenta, which is attached to the uterus, and then through the umbilical cord into the baby's blood. So the baby gets all it needs without having to eat. How do you think it gets rid of what it doesn't need?

CHILD: It can't go to the bathroom.

PARENT: No, it can't. But it doesn't urinate or move its bowels when it's in the uterus. Can you think of why it doesn't need to?

CHILD: The umbilical cord?

PARENT: The umbilical cord. After the baby uses all the oxygen and nourishment it needs, the umbilical cord carries the carbon dioxide and waste back into the mother's blood, so that it can be cleansed through her kidneys and eliminated when she goes to the bathroom.

8

Putting It All Together— Level Six

By Level Six, which may begin as early as eleven or twelve, young adolescents have leaped the final hurdle to understand the principle of conception. For the first time they can assimilate the concept that two distinct entities, sperm and ovum, can become one qualitatively different and unique entity, the embryo. Instead of the Level Four Reporter's piecing together of two halves of a body or the Level Five Theoretician's belief that one sex contributes the preformed baby while the other plays merely a supporting role, Level Six requires an appreciation that the genetic materials are transformed in the process of uniting. Now they know that the baby has no material existence before sperm and ovum unite, and that both parents contribute the substance from which it grows.

Although they give exclusively physical explanations of conception and birth, Level Six thinkers are also aware of the moral and social aspects of reproduction. They are able to integrate physiology with emotion, religious teaching, and social convention, taking all into account but differentiating among the role and influence of each. Until this level, the various strands tended to get tangled; now they are woven into a fabric that coheres. While they may still make factual errors, these young philosophers' analysis of the process of reproduction is multidimensional and well reasoned. They have begun to use, in Piaget's terms, formal operational thinking.

The path from early questions to clear and accurate solutions is a long one. Along the way, the child runs into mental hurdles that encourage detours. The detours lead back to the obstacles they appeared to avoid. The child is again faced with the same demand for a mental jump, only now the approach is from an angle that makes the leap possible.

We saw that by Level Four the child has discarded the more fantastic, idiosyncratic theories. The Reporters' thinking is no longer precausal, but their "just the facts please" solutions are based on faith in the authority of adults and books. They cannot provide an explanation of the *necessity* for the facts that they dutifully repeat, and they resist suggestions to think their way through to why the things they describe as being so are so.

At Level Five thought has become more flexible. Children are now willing to imagine the possibilities inherent in a situation and dare to go beyond what they know to be true to explore what might be true. Although their solutions to the question of how people get babies are not completely accurate, their reasoning is more developed and effective than that of the Level Four children, who may make fewer "mistakes." Daring more, they sometimes fall short of the mark, but the exercise improves their capacity to eventually reach their destination. The next step is the realization that the "baby" begins its physical existence only when the genetic materials from both parents have joined and that the traits derived from each are not assembled by the addition of discrete parts. Contrary to popular usage, the child is not a simple composite of "her mother's eyes," "her grandfather's nose," and "her father's temper." More-abstract thinking, Piaget's formal operations, may be necessary for Level Six explanations of the origin of babies that reflect children's appreciation of these distinctions.

The last great leap in cognitive development means that people no longer need think only in terms of real objects or concrete events, for they can carry on operations on symbols in their minds. They can reason on the basis of verbal propositions, as well as on the basis of things they can see and touch. They now know, for example, that if Joan is taller than Susan and Joan is shorter than Ellen, then Ellen is the tallest of the three. To figure this out, the thinker must be capable of reversing relationships (from "Joan is taller than Susan" to "Susan is shorter than Joan") and ordering the relationships one at a time or in chains.

For the first time, they can reflect on their own thought. They can develop theories and test them against reality and can think about thinking. Confronted with events and attitudes that are not easily interpreted within their existing ideologies, they see the contradictions as a call to reevaluate both the evidence and their own beliefs. They begin to be concerned that their beliefs be consistent and that their actions match their ideas and values. To examine beliefs in sets for internal inconsistency requires the ability to consider several rules or relationships at once. No longer limited to one-at-a-time analysis, they can think about events as having many dimensions, some of which may not be immediately apparent. The Level Three In-Betweens and Level Four Reporters were confused about the role of love and marriage in making babies, sometimes thinking that love was a material ingredient forming part of the baby's body or that special words said during the church service enabled the newlyweds to become parents. At Level Six, their ability to analyze the multiple dimensions of an event allows them to consider the emotional and social factors in parenthood without distorting the physiology of reproduction.

No longer is the truth absolute and mechanistic. The context of an event contributes to its meaning. Earlier a lie was always bad; now a lie that saves a life may be seen as virtuous. Before, a child could think that a hostile attack had to be the direct result of his own immediate action or a reflection that he is bad or unloved; now, the motive for the assault can be located in events that occurred in another time and place.

Able to distinguish between their own mental constructions and the world they know with their senses, formal operational thinkers are aware that their own experience is only a small sample of what is logically possible. If you tell a child, "Let's suppose coal is white," you can expect that child to protest, "But coal is black." Before they are about twelve years of age, children will refuse to consider problems with hypothetical premises that contradict reality, such as: If all winged cats are green, and I have a winged cat, what color is my cat? The younger child cannot disregard the evidence of his senses long enough to recognize and appreciate that the problem creates a self-contained world governed by its own internal rules. If an adolescent is told, "There are three schools, Roosevelt, Kennedy, and Lincoln schools, and three girls, Mary, Sue, and Jane, who go to different schools. Mary goes to the Roosevelt school, and Jane goes to the Kennedy school. Where does Sue go?" she answers, "Lincoln." The eight-year-old might say, however, "Sue goes to the Roosevelt school, because my sister has a friend called Sue and that's the school she goes to." (Kagan.)

The ability to formulate and make deductions from hypotheses that are contrary to fact liberates thinking about relations and classifications from their concrete and intuitive ties. Systematic problem-solving becomes possible only when all the possible solutions are considered and tried. Formal operations allow the thinker to combine propositions and isolate factors in order to confirm or disprove his belief. Piaget devised a task to assess whether children had acquired these mental capacities. Each child was asked to determine what factors determine the speed of movement (or "period") of a pendulum. Several possibilities were considered: length of the pendulum, the amount of weight attached, the height from which it was dropped, and the force with which it was originally set in motion. Concrete operational thinkers varied more than one factor at a time, frequently concluding that weight is a determining factor. Only the formal operational children held other factors constant as they varied one, trying different lengths with the same weight, for example, until they reached the correct solution. (Weight, height of drop, and original impetus are irrelevant. Only the length of the pendulum influences the speed of movement.) Verbal knowledge of science or physics did not help these young experimenters. Their own level of logical functioning was the key to a successful solution.

Level Six answers to the question about the origin of babies seem to require formal operations. Level Five is a transitional period between the concrete operations of Level Four and the more abstract thought possible at Level Six. But formal operations are not universal. While some children become concrete operational as early as five and others as late as nine or ten, everyone eventually does achieve this level of problem-solving. This is not true of formal operations. In a study of lower-middle- and upper-middle-class California residents, formal reasoning was used by 45 percent of the ten-to-fifteen-year-olds, 53 percent of the sixteen-to-twenty-year-olds, 65 percent of the twenty-one-to-thirty-year-olds, and 57 percent of the forty-five-to-fifty-year-olds. This means that these mental skills begin to be acquired about puberty, may not be established until adulthood, and for a large proportion are never fully developed. Not simply a matter of tested intelligence, with which is it not systematically related, formal reasoning arises only when maturation, social learning, and life experience both permit and require complex, abstract thought.

Recognizing that the embryo begins its biological existence at the moment of conception because both parents contribute genetic materials to its creation is the key to understanding Level Six thinking about reproduction. Children's explanations for the necessity of fertilization ranged from detailed, technical accounts to the vaguer "the fluids have to be together to make the baby" and "the two cells are attracted to each other, meet, and start growing." Regardless of whether the explanations are accurate, what is important is the felt need to seek reasons for the union of sperm and ovum, neither of which is said to contain a preformed baby.

Twelve-year-old Richard began his account of how people get babies by describing sexual intercourse: "Well, the male injects sperm into the female's womb, and an egg forms, and there you have a baby. Well, an egg is fertilized, and it grows into a fetus, which, after nine months of living in the womb, emerges as a baby."

According to Richard, fertilization was necessary to produce a chemical reaction between the sperm and the egg, a reaction that begins the embryo's development. Although he used an agricultural metaphor in defining fertilization, he made a distinction between plants and people: "Let's see, we talked about it in science. Fertilize means to help grow. To start the growth process, like when you fertilize your garden with fertilizer. It's to make it grow."

"Is the same kind of fertilizing with the egg as with the garden?" I asked.

"It's kind of hard to put. Yeah, it's different. When the egg is fertilized it sort of comes to life. If you want to . . . the chemicals make it come to life. The sperm are injected to where the eggs are, and they just, I guess, coat them. There's some chemical in the sperms that activates another chemical in the egg, which starts the development of the baby."

Mitchell's account was the most scientifically accurate description of conception. At thirteen, his knowledge was considerable. Despite his emphasis on detailed physiological events, he began by underlining the emotional context for making babies: "Well, first of all it's a relationship between two people. And so they decide they want to have a new person in their life. And so they decide that if they are going to have a baby, then they arrange to have intercourse. And so they, it takes place sometimes when they feel like they want to have intercourse so they have it. And then it takes a while, nine months is the usual time, but it can be born prematurely or after. So the baby's born, grows up, and so you have a baby and that's about it."

"How is the baby born?" I asked, unprepared for the detail that followed.

"Well, the male has two testicles, and they contain a substance known as semen, which carries the sperm, and it travels through this tube. I forget what the tube is. And it is pumped through the penis into the vagina of the girl, which in this time it goes in and embeds itself. Oh, I'm sorry. The sperm encounters one ovum, and one sperm breaks into the ovum which produces, the sperm makes like a cell, and the cell separates and divides, and so it's dividing, and the ovum goes through a tube and embeds itself in the wall of the, I think it's the fetus of the woman."

Mitchell's substitution of "fetus" for "uterus" underlines an important point. It is the sophistication of the child's reasoning, not simply whether his explanation is correct, that indicates the level of his understanding. Mitchell's verbal error is like the error of an algebra student who understands quadratic equations but makes a mistake in multiplication.

The only child I talked with to mention cell division forming the embryo, Mitchell also outlined the entire maturational process, complete with all the physiological changes experienced by both sexes at puberty. I had asked him how mothers get to be mothers.

"Well, they mature at a certain age. They start maturing basically at the age of, females mature before males, basically they're mature more quick than males. They start maturing at the age of about eleven to thirteen, and they just keep maturing. And they grow much taller, and they perspire, that's when you start perspiring more heavily, when you mature. And you grow hairs on different places, like under the arms and on the vagina and so forth. And that comes from maturing. And the breasts grow slowly, sometimes faster than usual. They grow from about twelve up, and then you stop growing at about . . . oh, I can't remember. But anyhow that's mostly part of it."

The question about how fathers get to be fathers, drew a parallel response: "Well, it's the same process. They mature, more slowly than females. They grow hairs under their arms and on their penis and around there. They perspire more heavily, and, oh yes, acne. You sometimes start getting acne as you mature, as you get older. And as they grow up, if they have intercourse then they produce the baby. And then they start to be a father, and they have to have responsibilities such as taking care of the baby and so forth."

He then went on to discuss various means of preventing conception. When I asked him if people not using contraceptives will have a baby following intercourse, he considered several factors: "After you're old, I mean very, if you're getting very old, you just stop producing, you always produce sperm but the sperm are just too weak, and they don't produce the right way and so nothing happens, you know. Contraceptive devices like vasectomy, which means you can have intercourse without using any other contraceptive like birth-control pills, you know."

"You talked about old people," I said. "What about young people?"

"Well, it depends on how young they are. You see you start producing sperm sometimes at thirteen, fourteen, fifteen, you just can't tell. See, if you were to have intercourse at thirteen, there are probabilities that you might, something might happen, the sperm might reach the egg, if there *are* any sperm, sometimes there aren't. And so that makes it very probable because sometimes people produce faster than others. There are just so many different people in the world, maturing differently than others."

Listening to Mitchell, the strength and availability of sperm seemed to be the only factor determining whether conception would occur. I tried to find out if he could think of any other reasons why intercourse without contraception may not lead to fertilization. I asked him, "If people are mature, do they have a baby every time they have intercourse?"

"Well, it depends really, because one time if you have intercourse you might have triplets or quadruplets or something, and you might, well yes, I think so, because you're producing sperm all the time, billions and billions of sperm, you're producing inside you. Producing in cells, like I mean they're cells themselves. So, you know it's probably that every time you have intercourse something might happen. But lots, a third, probably a third of the people use contraceptive devices, and I mean they only have to have intercourse even once or twice, unless you want to have a lot of children, you know. Most people don't have actual intercourse, for the child, more than twice or three times usually. Because they, you know, they can't afford to have that many kids. So they just use contraceptive devices if they want to have intercourse again. They would want to anyway, you know. Sometimes, you know, people do it sometimes just for the pleasure of it. They enjoy it."

Like others of his age, Mitchell knows that sex is not just for making babies. But he is so entranced with the changes going on in his own body, the "billions and billions" of sperm that promise his own future fertility, that he does not shift his focus to consider when and why females are fertile. I was so overwhelmed by the extent of his knowledge, and the extensiveness of his replies, that I failed to ask him the critical question: Why does fertilization have to occur to produce a baby?

Tina's reply to that question revealed that she learned about genes at school. Almost twelve when I talked with her, she lacked confidence in her answer, which was well thought out:

"Fertilization? Well, it just, it starts it off, I guess. You know. Well, mixes something. Mixes the genes or, well, puts particles or something into the egg, to make it, you know, fertilized. And so it will, you know, have genes and different kinds of blood and stuff like that, I guess. Because if it didn't, it would be more like the mother, I guess. Genes are the things from the father and the mother, you know, and they put a little bit of each into the baby, so the baby turns out to be a little bit like the mother or father or something. Not always, but a little bit."

Like Mitchell, she focused on her own sex in explaining why intercourse does not always lead to conception. He talked about the strength and number of sperm and the ages at which men produced them, while she centered, more accurately, on the availability of the egg: "They don't get a baby every time. It may be, like the middle of the month or something like that. Well, then the mother's not having her menstruation, and she can have a baby. But when she is, the egg can't be fertilized. Because it's just not in the right place or something like that. Or it's taken out. But when the egg is fertilized, it begins to grow and get bigger, to become a person, a baby, and then it gets big enough so that it comes out."

Both Mitchell and Tina show that even bright, knowledgeable, precocious early adolescents may not take into consideration all the factors leading to conception. In this way, they differ little from many adults. But what is most striking in their accounts of conception and birth is the absence of wonder. Naive and wanting to appear grown up, they keep any anxiety under control by talking about reproduction in terms of technicalities. The awe of the young child who sees birth as magical has gone underground, to surface again in the expectant parent. Few of the older children are ingenuous enough to admit that the facts they have worked so hard to understand are wonderful as well as true.

Physiology, love, marriage, religion, and the stork all figure in twelve-year-old Donna's account of sex and birth. More than any other child I spoke with, she was able to give each its due, recognizing the influence and weight of each factor without blending or confusing them. When I asked her how people get babies, she replied:

"Well, do you want the main thing? Well, they have sexual

intercourse. And then the mother, when the egg is developed enough, she becomes pregnant by not having her period. And then she knows, and goes to a doctor, and they have all these tests. Then nine months the baby is developing, and by the seventh month, the baby can kick, it sucks its thumb and does things that it would usually do outside. And it can be born by seven months, but it is rather little. And by eight months the doctor usually says not to go anywhere out of Berkeley, out of wherever you live, not anyplace else. And by nine months you're supposed to stay really close to home. And you can't expect it on the exact date, but any time around that. Then the baby is born."

I asked her to define some of the words she used.

"Born means beginning a new life, or can mean beginning anything, I guess. The baby comes down a tube that opens down the vagina, and it's born!

"Pregnant means having somebody, something inside you, I guess. A baby.

"Sexual intercourse? Well, it should only be brought on by love, and it helps if you're married. And it's when the man and the woman come together, and the man sticks his penis into the lady's, near the womb, and then the egg that comes down through a little tube, down into the womb, is fertilized, and becomes a child."

Donna's description of fertilization uses an agricultural analogy to describe how children inherit their parents' traits. Her vivid images contrast with her hazy concept of what genes are all about: "Well, I guess it's just something that the man . . . Oh, wait, yeah, I know. All the things, like things that are going to be put into the baby, like what color hair it's going to be, if it's going to be curly and stuff, sort of like it gets fertilizer sprinkled on the little seed. It's sort of like the same idea, except instead of . . . bull . . . crap or whatever you might put on your plants, it's the genes, the way the baby's going to be after it's born. The genes are from the man and the woman. But when the man gives it to the woman, I guess it would be called the man fertilizing the woman." Clear that the egg "is not an embryo until it's fertilized," she had no preformist ideas.

Donna could take more than one perspective to look at the same events. Her theological explanation of the origin of babies in no way contradicted her description of the physiology of birth. Each point of view added to the full human story of how people feel and behave to reproduce their own kind. When I asked her, "What is it about sexual intercourse that starts a baby?" she answered from several angles:

"Um, the fertilizing part, I guess. The part that a man and a woman love each other enough to have a child and to bring it into the world. If you want to think of the part that's the truth, or the mechanical stuff about it, if you want to think of the mechanical thing, the mother makes it. I don't know exactly, but if you were religious you'd say that God put it there. If you're religious you think that God put it there, because He wants another child on the earth, and that your love sort of sends a message, telling Him that you want a child. And if you're little, you tell a kid that the stork brings it. I always figured that the stork was God, and He's putting the child there. I guess that's how the word that the stork brings it got around. But a woman can't have a baby without having sexual intercourse, because the man has organs in him that have to go, or be put together with the woman's organs. If they're not put together, it's impossible."

Sex, love, God's will, early-childhood birth tales, and physiology are all there. The role of each is kept distinct and then fitted together so that none overshadows or engulfs another, showing that her conceptual skills are formal operational.

Her reminiscences about earlier thinking on the subject had an engaging, fanciful quality, incorporating images typical of the Level One Geographers and the Level Two Manufacturers: "Cartoons have lots of ways, but they're always, you know, that the stork brings them. Since I didn't have any little brothers and sisters when I was little enough not to understand, I didn't think about it. I just thought, you know, that it happened. A baby was there. Nothing ever started or anything. So I guess I just figured that you were there from the beginning of time, you know. Well, and once I saw a Shirley Temple movie, and everybody was up in the air, and all of a sudden a boat came by and the man would call out names. One time there was a couple of lovers there, and they had to be separated. You know, you were a big person, you grew up there. And when you grew up you started all over again. By the time you got down to earth, you were a child. It was just kind of . . . it was confusing to me. I didn't get it, but I guess that's how I figured it happened." The muddled and magical views of early childhood, while delightful, had left her, in her own words, confused. Some of the other older children had similar memories.

I asked all the eleven- and twelve-year-olds to try to remember how they used to think about reproduction: "What did you think about how people get babies when you were little, before you understood it as well as you do now?" About two thirds of them could reconstruct the beliefs of earlier childhood, producing explanations that fit earlier levels in the sequence of stages I have been describing.

Ellen remembered believing that "babies just happened," and William "thought first that women just keep having babies and that birth control meant ways to keep them from getting them." James remembered thinking that babies were bought at the store. Although no child I spoke with, of any age, confessed to believing that storks delivered babies, three of the older children said that they used to think so when they were little. Kevin qualified this, stating, "I probably thought about the stork, that the stork brought them to the hospital probably." He thought he was four at the time. Tina remembered giving the doctor the critical role in conception, thinking that "the doctor had to do something to the mother at a certain time of the month."

Two children remembered thinking that a baby was a

physical expression of the love between its parents. Susan believed that kissing produced babies, and Tessa, more abstractly, said, "I always thought that people were so much in love with each other that they just had babies, sort of like a reward or something for being in love with each other."

Karl recalled believing in the digestive fallacy, confusing conception with eating and birth with elimination: "I think I thought that it grew up in her stomach from eating something special, and it came out when you shit in the toilet. I guess I was five or six then."

Jean, at twelve, described her beliefs about birth when she was six: "I thought that they went to a hospital, and the doctor put some medicine on the belly button, and the belly button would open up, and they'd take the baby out. And then they'd put the medicine back on, and it would close up, and then they'd have the baby."

Robert's memories were vivid. When I asked him if he remembered what he used to think, he answered in detail: "Yes, I do. My sister said, 'I'm going to have a baby when I grow up.' And I said, 'You might not, it all happens by chance.' You know, all of a sudden, just BOOM, it comes out! I thought, see, my parents are lucky to have three kids. How come humans are so lucky that we have so many people in the world. I never learned, my mother and my father never told me about the birds and the bees, so, I went to school and I never got taught it. I just learned it from other kids. And then I got all my ideas changed. See, I had all these weird ideas about how you just got born by chance. You just quickly came out. Like when your mother goes to the bathroom, all of a sudden a baby falls out. And that's exactly what I thought. It's weird!"

These sixth- and seventh-graders find their earlier beliefs alien, "weird," and incomprehensible. Like adults, they have achieved some distance from their childhood ways of thinking and, having developed new problem-solving strategies and modes of thought, see the old ideas as so many cast-off, outgrown clothes, useless, amusing, or embarrassing—"Did I ever fit in that?"

Talking with Level Five Children

In talking to Level Four Reporters and Level Five Theoreticians the objective is the same, although the Level Four child may take longer to understand why genetic material must unite to produce a baby. The Level Five child believes that the whole baby exists in either sperm or ovum, needing the other only to promote its growth. Children at these levels can be introduced to the idea that the baby has not begun to exist until the sperm and ovum meet and fuse. They can learn that the seeds of life come from both parents, from whom the baby inherits its physical characteristics.

A useful way to explain genetic contributions is to talk in terms of information. A parent might say that both sperm and ovum contain coded information about the baby they will grow to be. He can go on to talk about facial features, color of eyes, hair, and skin. It is important to stress that neither the sperm nor the ovum has the entire code until they unite. Together, they complete the message to develop into a baby that is the child of a particular set of parents.

For example, let's consider a conversation with a child who holds the Level Five theory that the baby is "really" in the sperm, needing the ovum only to feed and house the sperm as it develops into an embryo. A parent might encourage the child to speculate further:

PARENT: That's an interesting theory. Do you know what a theory is?

CHILD: Does it mean something that's not true?

PARENT: No, a theory is an idea about how something happens that seems to fit the facts. It's an educated guess, by someone who's thought hard about the problem and has an idea that makes sense. A theory can be true, and a theory can be untrue. And sometimes we don't have enough evidence to decide.

CHILD: Is my theory true?

PARENT: No, but it's a very good theory just the same. Not so long ago some of the very best scientists in the world thought about it just as you do. It wasn't until they had very powerful microscopes, so they could study how things happened very carefully, that they found out more about it. Can you think what they might have found?

CHILD: Was the baby really in the ovum?

PARENT: What do you think?

CHILD: I don't think so.

PARENT: You're right, it isn't. One way to think our way to how the baby is first formed is to think about how babies get to look the way they do, each one different. How do you suppose some babies get to have blue eyes and some babies are born with brown eyes?

CHILD: I know. From their mother and father. I have red hair like Mommy, and everyone says my face looks just like yours, Daddy.

PARENT: I think so too. So if you grew from a sperm, it would be pretty hard to understand how you got all that red hair.

CHILD: Something from Mommy must have got into me too. Something from the ovum, I guess.

PARENT: Uh-huh. Do you know what a code is?

CHILD: Sure, that's special writing so only your friends know what you're saying. Little squiggles or numbers and things.

PARENT: Well, our bodies use a code to tell the baby how to develop. We call the little bits of coded information "genes." There are genes that determine hair and skin and eye color, how tall we grow, whether our hair will be straight or curly, and lots of other things about how we look and how we'll grow. But each ovum and each sperm has only half the genes needed to start a baby. Until the sperm and the ovum join together, there isn't enough information about how to form a baby. When they're together, the code is complete and the message is to develop into a baby that is the child of this particular mother and father. Each baby is a new combination of their genes, so it looks a little like both but exactly like neither.

CHILD: So the baby is *really* from both parents.

PARENT: Sure. We each get half of our genes from our mother and her ancestors and the other half from our father and his family. Neither the sperm nor the ovum can determine how the baby will grow on its own. But when they join together, they don't just get bigger, they form something entirely new: an embryo that will grow to be a baby.

Parents may want to include a discussion of how genes are arranged along tiny threadlike chromosomes in the nuclei of the sperm and ovum. Knowing that sperm and ova have only twenty-three chromosomes, while all other human cells have forty-six, gives children a mathematical handle on the concept that neither sperm nor ovum is complete and capable of generating new life on its own.

As they enter adolescence, children begin to think more about sexual matters, anticipating beginning to date and having to make decisions about how to behave sexually. Parents will probably want to be clear with their adolescent children about what their own standards of sexual morality are—and why they feel the way they do. Young people are more likely to adopt their parents' values when they understand that those values come from careful consideration of the issue and real concern for their children's growth and happiness, rather than fear and the arbitrary exercise of parental power. Only values which the adolescents have made their own, internalizing their parents' respect for them as self-respect, will have a lasting effect on their actions.

Information about conception and contraception do not encourage young people toward premature sexual activity. And ignorance is no deterrent. When one out of five babies born in the United States this year will have a mother who is not yet seventeen, withholding information about contraception from teenagers is ridiculous. Because they can now differentiate between the physical, social, and moral aspects of sexual behavior, young people can (if they want to) understand that conception is possible even if the prospective parents (a) don't want a baby, (b) are not in love, and (c) are having sexual intercourse for the first time.

Talking about reproduction with young adolescents might well include thinking together about why people have children, as well as how they have babies. Parents will probably want to emphasize the importance of intention and planning in having children when one is ready to take care of them and help them grow. As with more factual matters, questions of value require that the discussion be a dialogue rather than a lecture. Young people are more likely to put into practice values that they participate in formulating. And lecturers are less likely to be consulted in time of doubt and confusion than people who state their positions clearly and who are truly responsive to the young person's feelings and thoughts.

9

And What about the Parents?

During the past four years, I have talked about children's ideas about how people get babies with many groups of parents and teachers. Everywhere I found attentive adult audiences, eager to learn more about how children think so that they might better communicate with the children in their lives. Early in each discussion, however, the topic shifted to another active issue for these adults: How should they respond to children's sexual behavior at school or at home? Not wanting to create guilt or feelings of unworthiness in the children, they were left with their own discomfort and the nagging feeling that some limits were appropriate. They knew that they did not want to repeat the negative messages about sexuality that they themselves had received in childhood, but, lacking positive examples, they felt unsure as to where to draw the line. And they didn't know what to do with their own feelings of discomfort, distaste, or avoidance.

So I found myself leading discussions on a subject about which I felt like a journeyman carpenter trying to construct a house from three sets of sketchy plans. I had done some thinking about childhood sexuality, but I felt less than expert on the subject. In speaking to these groups and learning from the experience of those most actively concerned with what to do on a daily basis, my own thoughts and feelings became clearer.

I'd like to discuss here some of the questions that kept

popping up again and again as I reported on my research. For a more extensive discussion of how to feel more confident in your response to childhood sexuality, I recommend Sol Gordon's *Let's Make Sex a Household Word* and Wardell Pomeroy's *Your Child and Sex.*

Masturbation

Attitudes toward masturbation have changed drastically since World War I. Even Margaret Sanger, the noted birth-control pioneer, wrote at that time that masturbation should be discouraged as causing permanent bodily harm. Blindness, sterility, warts, madness, and the waste of needed sperm were all blamed on that ubiquitous demon, masturbation. Given the prevalence of the activity so maligned, the only question is how our forebears explained how so many people remained sighted and sane.

Gradually medical science acknowledged that these dire allegations were unfounded, as many had already discovered from personal experience. Until recently, informed opinion on the subject was that masturbation was not harmful. But recent evidence goes further, to assert that it is a sign of healthy normality with long-term benefits as well as short-term pleasures.

As early as 1905, Freud wrote that the sexual instinct is aroused by maternal affection as well as by direct excitation of the genitals. He asked mothers not to blame themselves for the sexual impact of their tender nurturance:

"She is only fulfilling her task in teaching the child to love. After all, he is meant to grow up into a strong and capable person with vigorous sexual needs and to accomplish during his life all the things that human beings are urged to do by their instincts."

Later research supported this connection between overt genital sexuality in infants and the quality of the mothering they receive. René Spitz observed infants throughout their first year of life. His findings were impressive. Of the babies

who received virtually no nurturance, none displayed any
genital masturbation, even though they received all the usual
stimulation involved in ordinary diapering and bathing. Those
whose mothers had personal problems that hindered the
quality of the care they offered showed some self-stimulation
but no genital masturbation. The babies given the best
maternal care all began to masturbate by their first birthday,
even without unusual genital stimulation. The study concludes that infantile sexuality develops spontaneously in the
presence of quality nurturance, clearly demonstrating that it
is both normal and healthy. (Gadpaille.)

Masturbation provides very necessary learning about one's
own body, what it's like and how it works. Familiarity with
how one's body functions sexually is important to adult
sexual pleasure. The Kinsey studies of sexual behavior found
that women are more likely to have orgasms during intercourse after marriage if they have had orgasms, by whatever
means, before. Most of the sex therapists I know who work
with preorgasmic women have also noted that most of the
women coming for treatment report little or no masturbatory
experience.

It is important not to discourage children from this very
necessary exploration of their own bodies. Even if you are
unconvinced that it has a positive role in the child's developing sexuality, trying to stop it does no good. A study by
Landis and others revealed that prohibitions and threats
against masturbation produced guilt but did not lessen the
frequency of the behavior they were designed to eliminate.

For most parents the question is how to deal with their
own old conflicts so that they don't pass on restrictive, in-
hibiting messages to their children. Parents, too, have feelings that they need to respect. In Chapter 2 I discussed
some of the consequences of running roughshod over one's
own sensibilities. If you are merely paying lip service to a
more enlightened standard than you can actually embrace,
your child will mirror your conflict. Commenting on the

gap between what you know to be right and your own feelings can help children be clear with themselves.

Knowing they don't want to repeat the often well-intentioned mistakes of their own fathers and mothers, many parents today are trying to be more responsive to their children's needs. They learn that frowning or saying "Don't" leaves the shamed child feeling "I'm bad." Trying to distract the masturbating child with a toy or the suggestion of another activity does not avoid the implied criticism.

This does not mean that parents cannot or should not put limits on their children's masturbation or other sexual activity. By the time children are three or four, they can be taught that it is not good manners to masturbate in public. Preschool children, even toddlers, have already learned that there are appropriate times and places for many of their activities: Eating is done at the table, sleeping in the bedroom, elimination in the toilet, painting in a special part of the nursery. Masturbation need not be treated differently. A parent can tell her child, as did a woman quoted by Lonnie Barbach, "I know it feels good to play with your penis and it's OK, but it makes me uncomfortable when you do it here in the living room. I would feel much better if you would go in your bedroom, where you can have privacy." In this way, this mother acknowledges that the child's good feeling is appropriate and respected, but she also takes care of her own feelings of discomfort. Because she takes responsibility for what she feels, requesting that he move to another room for her benefit, she does not lead him to confuse her needs with his own. When space is more limited, parents and children will need more ingenuity to assure that each person has some time to be alone.

Children need confirmation that touching one's genitals is supposed to feel good, that pleasure is one aspect of having sexual organs, and that others have had the same experience. People usually begin to masturbate in infancy and may continue throughout their lives. It is not "babyish" to masturbate, although with children who are no longer babies some discretion about time and place and respect for the feelings and values of others are expected. Boys need to know that their erections are a normal part of male sexuality, and both sexes would be better prepared to understand their own bodies if they were told that "sometimes a special feeling called orgasm can occur." (Barbach.) Kinsey found that 21 percent of the males and 12 percent of the females he interviewed had masturbated to orgasm by age twelve, figures that were elevated to 82 percent and 20 percent, respectively, by age fifteen.

Until recently, parents erred by being overly restrictive toward children's masturbation. Although still in the minority, some parents today are swinging too far with the proverbial pendulum, exhorting their children to masturbate. The problem with this approach is that masturbation is something children should do for their own pleasure, not to please their parents. What is a delight if discovered by themselves can become a duty if done at their parents' direction. It is important for children to feel that their bodies belong to themselves alone. To try to program a child to masturbate intrudes on her self-control and self-direction. According to Pomeroy, "the best a parent can do is to give the child privacy, refrain from embarrassing him or instilling him with guilt and fear, and answer his questions when and if he asks them."

One further question remains: How much masturbation is "too much"? In this context, "too much" usually means "more than I do." But compulsive masturbation can begin as early as toddlerhood. Like any other compulsive behavior, such as involuntary overeating, oversleeping, incessant talking or hitting, compulsive masturbation is a sign of emotional conflict. If it is short-lived and the only symptom of distress, it is seldom serious.

How can you tell if masturbation is excessive or compulsive? Gadpaille defines a compulsive activity as one that occurs "so repetitively and incessantly as to interfere with other normal activities. One example is the child who might normally be expected to be fascinated by a new toy, playing with a friend, or enjoying a birthday party, but who seems totally preoccupied with manipulating his genitals. By focusing on the feeling in his penis, this child can withdraw his attention from the real world, giving himself the pleasure and comfort he requires without having to look outside himself toward a reality that feels frustrating." Gadpaille endorses parents' concern in such cases, pointing out that the compulsive masturbation that produces more tension than it relieves "is a symptom (not a cause) of some emotional difficulty. The difficulty can be discovered only by study of the particular child, but parents might generally try to be alert to whatever could be overtaxing the youngster's limited ego capacity to cope, such as the arrival of a new sibling, the loss of someone or something important, or a new environmental demand, such as toilet training or nursery school, for which the child is not quite ready or which may be presented too forcefully." Often parents can determine what is distressing the child and either change the situation or give the child new skills with which to cope.

Sex Play

Ellen is sitting at the kitchen table finishing her coffee and reading the newspaper. From the bathroom she hears the voices of her six-year-old son and five-year-old daughter, who are sharing a tub. "Let's play sex," one proposes. "Now let's try penis to butt." Ellen is bewildered. Should she go in there and get them out of the tub quickly? Or is this harmless fun she can afford to ignore?

Jeanne is playing with her four-year-old daughter, Amy. Amy bounces on Jeanne's knee and slides down her leg, climbing back on mother's lap for more. Jeanne realizes that Amy's pleasure is sexual and becomes uncomfortable and embarrassed. She wants to stop the game without giving Amy the impression she is doing something wrong.

Peter and Jenny are four. They lie down in the corner of the nursery school, hug each other, and thrust their pelvises together. The teachers look at each other, each hoping the other will do something to stop the children, but neither wanting to have to handle the situation herself.

"What on earth am I supposed to do now?" is the feeling many adults have upon seeing children's play take an explicitly sexual turn. Profoundly aware of their own embarrassment and discomfort, and not wanting to handicap their children with anxious, angry, or punitive prohibitions, they waver at the starting line, acting uncertainly, hesitating to intervene, or impulsively jumping in to let off their own steam.

Ellen allowed her children to finish their bath uninterrupted, but she was left with lingering doubts about whether this was a dereliction of maternal duty. Jeanne told Amy that she was uncomfortable playing the leg-sliding game and wanted to stop. After a brief hesitation, one of the nursery-school teachers told Peter and Jenny that their play was not a game to be played at school and attempted to divert their attention to a new activity.

You may have handled each of these situations differently from the adults described. There is no one right way to respond that rules out the alternatives. What you choose to do will have to take into account both the child's welfare and your own sensibilities. We have already seen how parents who discount their own feelings, acting as they think they "should" without acknowledging some of their own conflicts, can give double messages that trap their children in pitfalls they had hoped to avoid.

The beginning journalists' instruction to find out who, what, where, when, and why, can also be of service to the parent trying to assess when and how to respond to children's sexual play. Who is participating, what they are doing, where and when and why they have chosen to do it all enter into determining the appropriate adult response.

WHO

California recently passed legislation decriminalizing the private sexual activities of consenting adults. The principle behind this relaxation of legal restrictions is that people should be able to determine how they wish to behave so long as they neither exploit another person nor inflict their own standards of behavior on an unwilling audience. Although not directly applicable to children, the same philosophy can inform our judgments about children's sexual play.

Who is playing with whom? Are they equals, peers whose interests and capacities are developmentally matched? Or is one older, bigger, stronger, and able to use these advantages to intimidate or coerce the other? Is the activity something they are doing *with* each other, sharing the initiative and direction of the play, or is one doing something *to* the other, making up all the rules and leaving the other to feel acted upon rather than fully participant?

Gadpaille writes: "Children playing freely within groups of peers will interact, whether sexually or in any other way, at the level of their own spontaneous readiness. With the exception of older bullies ganging up on one or more younger children—a situation akin to child-adult sexuality—little children will express interest according to their own levels of ego and erotic development. Those who are not ready will not participate."

According to researchers (Ford and Beach, Money and Hampson), permissiveness toward sexual play in childhood leads to more enjoyment of sexuality and fewer sexual problems as adults. "Many people reared in our culture," writes Gadpaille, "pay a high personal price for the supposed rewards of sexual repression, the price being alienation from one's sexual self, diminished capacity for tenderness and human closeness, a high incidence of sexual conflicts and disordered function, and perhaps the inability to think and feel like a whole person or to relate to others wholly." He concludes that "the evidence available to date is balanced in favor of relaxing the strictures against childhood sex play, both privately and with other children."

This does not extend to direct sexual activity with adults or older children, which is most often emotionally detrimental. While experts do differ about when to restrict children's sex play, clinical evidence and informed professional opinion are strongly opposed to adult-child sexual activity. There is no way for adults and children to partake in sexual activity that is respectful of the child's immature level of development. There can be no mutuality when the difference in power is so substantial. Children are in no position to freely give their informed consent to an activity determined by the more urgent sexual needs of an adult. Having learned that adults are to be obeyed, and aware of their own puny strength, they cannot be the ones to set the limits. When what is happening is more stimulating than children can handle, they typically regress to earlier, less conflict-filled times in their own lives, behaving in age-inappropriate, immature ways.

Most adults want to protect children from premature overstimulation. Parents, especially, want to make their homes safe places in which children can grow, supported by adult guidance but directed by their own development needs. When parents begin to experience sexual feelings for their own children, they react with alarm and shame. Because people seldom talk about these very secret feelings, they do not realize that sexual fantasies about one's children are common. It is normal to feel turned on by warm, affectionate, sensual little people. Acting out the fantasies could hurt the children, but having them is both normal and harmless.

Typically, parents having sexual feelings or fantasies about their children will do something to put more distance between them and the child. Picking a fight with the child reassures the parent that his feared and shameful thoughts will stay just thoughts. In *Games People Play,* Eric Berne called this maneuver "Uproar." It is marked by mutual fault-finding and raised voices. The anger of this game helps players avoid their sexual feelings, slamming bedroom doors to emphasize the limits to their intimacy. It is especially popular between fathers and their teenage daughters, but can take place between parent and child of either sex from preschool on. While this way of retreating from sexual feelings may reduce the possibility of acting them out, there are less-destructive ways of assuring the same result. Even when children are their most seductive, adults can set limits without either rejecting them or mystifying the issues to produce distance.

I was recently told of a nursery-school teacher who complained to the mother of one of the four-year-old girls in his class that her daughter was being too sexual with him. He was adamant without being explicit about what she had actually done, but he had refused her access to his lap. My guess is that he was feeling aroused by her (unspecified) behavior and, anxious about his own sexual feelings, was trying to sever the affectional tie between them. How much better for her if he had been able to set limits without cutting her off entirely. As a youngster exploring her own sexuality and men's responses to her, her need was to feel that she could be sexual without either getting in beyond her depth or alienating his affection. If, for example, she had been fondling his penis—the most extreme of the possibilities—he might have said: "I want you to be able to sit in my lap when you feel like it, but I don't want you to touch my penis. It makes me uncomfortable when you do that, so I can't allow it." He can restrict the behavior he finds unacceptable without making her feel bad about herself or the expression of sexuality.

In limiting children's sexual play, adults are called upon to exercise discretion, delicacy, and compassion. Emotional outbursts and threats may scare children into submission, but the guilt, shame, and fear left in their wake are often more disturbing than the events that occasioned such responses. Most parents want to teach their children to respect other people's wishes, rejecting coercion or exploitation as means of getting your own way. Overwhelming children with explosives tirades works against this important value. We may say "Do as I say, not as I do," but our practice is more convincing than our theory.

One obvious time when limits are called for is when sexual playmates are not peers. Children can be taught about older bullies who may take advantage of them in nonsexual as well as sexual ways. But who is involved is not the only issue in determining whether parental restrictions are in the child's best interests. What is going on is another criterion.

WHAT

Mutual exploration is an important part of early-childhood learning. Curiosity about the sexual equipment of the other half of the world is both natural and normal, and many nursery schools now have open bathrooms so that children can find out more about sexual differences in an uncontrived, everyday way. Even play that involves direct genital stimulation, if it occurs between peers whose parents have similarly permissive values, can be harmless. But parents do need to be alert to whether children are being overstimulated in sex play.

There is no guideline that answers that question for every child alike. Most parents have learned to recognize when their children are overtired. Even if children protest that they are not sleepy, parents can tell by their high-pitched tones or restless overactivity that it's time to go to bed. In the same way, only knowing your child, how she behaves when she is feeling happy or angry or sick or silly or tired, gives you the background to judge if she is overstimulated by sex play. Typically, children who are overstimulated will regress, acting more "babyish" when they have ventured beyond their developmental depth. Nursery-school teachers, who may expect and encourage comments and observations on sex differences by children, know that when the remarks get too silly, it's time to turn their attention to another topic.

WHERE AND WHEN

Where and when the play is taking place is another issue to consider in deciding when to discourage children's sex play. Wandering into a child's room and observing a game of "Doctor" in progress, a mother may choose to say "Excuse me" and close the door, teaching the children that their privacy is respected. The same mother might tell them to put on some clothes and find another game to play if she encountered the same behavior on the sidewalk or at Grandma's house. As with masturbation, and so many other things, children can easily learn that there are different times and places for different activities.

Sometimes children choose times and places for sexual play that they know adults will find unacceptable. While they may enjoy testing the limits of the adults "in charge," children are usually reassured to find that adults can assert those limits. In the dominant American culture, direct sexual activity usually takes place in private. Even when this is not wholly possible, some attempt is made to maximize the privacy of the setting for sexual encounter. Children whose play is explicitly sexual while they are in the company of adults are usually testing how those adults will respond, aware that they may be making the grown-ups uncomfortable. Their choice of a public place is frequently an invitation for intervention. You can be sure that they are begging for limits if they appear more attentive to adult reactions than engrossed in their own exploration.

It is difficult to avoid making children feel ashamed of being sexual when the society in which we live is not comfortable with sexuality in general and childhood sexuality in particular. Parents can be an important source of reassurance that it is okay to enjoy the pleasures of the body, but they cannot maintain for their children the illusion that the greater society thinks as they do. Children will also learn, from opening their senses to the content of the cultural media (language, television, advertising, radio, films, and literature to name a few) and by playing and sharing ideas with other children, that there is something embarrassing and taboo about sex. Not until there is greater agreement that childhood sexuality is a natural part of children's developing knowledge of themselves and human experience will shame and furtiveness be replaced by unselfconscious expression.

Parents can help children deal with confusing and contradictory messages about sexuality from different sources by commenting on the differences. Articulating the unsaid reduces confusion. It is preferable to tell children that other people may disapprove of children's sex play than for them to sense that there is something wrong without knowing what. Their embarrassment and giggles in talking about sex or being observed in sex play by adults shows that they have picked up on adult discomfort, whether from their parents or the larger community. They need to hear that the discomfort is real but the activity that arouses it is not bad. One way to explain this is:

PARENT: Sometimes children get embarrassed about wanting to know more about sex. They can tell that grownups get uncomfortable when they talk about sex or see children playing sex. When grown-ups were children, people used to think differently about how to talk to children about sex. Even though they now know that it is important for children to be able to find out more about sex, sometimes the old feelings they learned when they were children get in the way of their feeling easy about it. Now they know that sex can be fun and feels good, but they feel more comfortable when people save their sex play for times when other people aren't there.

Many parents who would like to be more permissive about sex play between child peers worry about their children's playmates' going home to tell Mom or Dad that Jimmy's parents let them do what their own parents forbid. Children don't usually go home and tell. If sex play is forbidden at home, they're too afraid that their parents would be angry that they've transgressed. But the problem remains a delicate one. When playmates come from homes with different values, some discussion of these differences will help them navigate the confusion of diverging paths. Parents are usually called upon to explain why they feel differently from Jane's parents about television viewing, homework, good nutrition, spanking, fights, or politics. Differences about sex play can also be explained, simply, in terms of values. In a heterogeneous culture, children need to know the distinctions among fact, opinion, and value.

Nudity

To cover up or not to cover up in front of one's children is a question that makes many parents wonder. Some parents who enjoy and are used to being nude around the house worry that it might not be good for the children. Others, who are more comfortable when clothed, think that perhaps they should disrobe in front of their children as a laboratory session in sex education.

Parents' attitudes toward their own bodies have an important impact on their children's sexuality. If parents hide their bodies and are embarrassed upon being discovered unclothed, children will learn that there is something shameful about the human body. Casual and unaffected parental nudity conveys the message that parents are "at home" in their bodies, comfortable and self-accepting in being incarnate. Natural, matter-of-fact nudity in the home is beneficial to children, who will follow these models of comfortable self-acceptance. Not for them the shock at puberty reported to me by a young woman: "When I first got pubic hair, I thought I was turning into a monkey, 'cause I'd never seen an adult nude."

Parental nudity is sometimes thought to be overstimulating to children. I think it is the attitude of the adults, how they feel when they are undressed, and not the nudity itself that can be distressing. A look at other cultures shows us that nudity is not necessarily damaging to children. It is the emotional message the parent is broadcasting, not how many clothes he or she is wearing, that influences how children will feel. If parents are self-conscious about being undressed, they will transmit anxiety and doubt rather than comfortable self-assurance. If this is the case, parents can quietly request privacy, avoiding a show of distress.

Seductiveness, not nudity, is what overstimulates children. Parents can be seductive without being nude, and nude without being seductive. Nudity is not automatically seductive. It is natural and appropriate to be nude when dressing, in the bathroom, or when the family is relaxing at home. If family members are unselfconscious and matter-of-fact in their nudity, the sexual charge and excitement of exhibitionism that can be seductive and overstimulating to children will not be present. Children can tell whether parents are comfortably being themselves or making a big deal out of showing off.

Children will often let you know if they are uncomfortable with nudity in the home. Some may choose to wear clothes when others are nude, and this choice should be respected not mocked. Sometimes children who had earlier felt easy about going around the house without clothes begin to want more privacy about their bodies as they begin the changes of puberty. Parents can be sensitive to these changes in children's needs as they mature. Alert to signals of discomfort, they can ask, "Are you uncomfortable?" And if the answer is "Yes," "What can I do to make things easier for you?" It is better to ask than to jump to conclusions. One woman I spoke with remembered her own upset at abrupt shifts in the family culture: "In my house everybody ran around without clothes. When I was a preadolescent, my mother convinced my father that he should at least were underwear in in the bathroom when he was shaving. It seemed all of a sudden, and I remember it as a strange sort of feeling, real sad. All at once I felt separated from an intimacy I had felt with my family."

No matter how comfortable parents are about being nude, they cannot create a Trobriand Island in one household. One eight-year-old boy questioned his mother about her nude sunbathing in the back yard: "What are you going to do when I bring a friend over?" When she replied, "Lie here," he protested, "In front of my *friend?*" The choice before her was clear. She could either continue her sunbathing *au naturel*, exiling her son and his friends from the house, or set up a distant-early-warning system for him to alert her that the outside world was at the door, so that some agreed-upon accommodation could be put in effect. Only the second choice conveys to a child that his needs, too, are respected.

Witnessing Adult Sexuality

Children need to know that sex is for pleasure and emotional intimacy as well as for making babies. It is important that they see that their parents' love for each other has a physical side, too. Kissing, hugging, cuddling, and being generally affectionate with each other teaches children about love. Experts agree, however, that "in our culture this doesn't mean making love with the children as spectators or participants." In talking to mothers, Barbarch put it this way: "It might be good to let your child know that you and Daddy make love in the privacy of your bedroom; that during that time you don't like to be disturbed and any questions and problems can generally wait until afterward. To treat sex with dignity and love rather than to shroud it in awkward and unspeakable mystery is an excellent way of instilling a child with a healthy attitude toward sex."

There is no hard evidence that witnessing parental intercourse harms children, but most writers on the subject advocate caution. For most people the world over, during most historical periods, children have been exposed to adult sexual activity. It cannot, then, be inherently damaging. But what works in other times and places may not be optimal here and now. Gadpaille suggests that the criterion for whether this or any other practice is "benevolent" or "harmful" rests on "whether early sexual stimulation influences development in a direction" that is harmonious or divergent from later cultural expectations. While other cultures may provide ways for children to express their sexuality within the family, at this point in our history seeing adult intercourse may stimulate children without giving them an opportunity for discharging their excitement.

Overstimulation is a frequently given reason for parents to "take gentle pains to prevent children from intruding into their own intimacy or forcing their sexuality on them." (Gadpaille.) Equally important is the tendency of young children to misperceive adult sexuality as involving violence and mutilation. Children who "accidentally" open the bedroom door when parents are making love can easily conclude that Daddy is hurting Mommy. They have no anchor in their own experience to hold them to the idea that these are two people who love each other enjoying themselves. The passion, the insistent thrusting, facial expressions, and sounds of adult intercourse can appear more aggressive than tender. Gadpaille reports a three-and-a-half-year-old boy who cried out, "Don't 'pank Mommy!" and hit his father after inadvertently interrupting them during sexual intercourse.

When children have unlimited opportunities to witness adult sex, they cannot maintain their fearful misconceptions. Reality becomes a constant reminder that sex is not as dangerous as it may appear. For example, the child who sees the penis enter the vagina erect and exit flaccid may think that it has been damaged. After he has witnessed this cycle repeated time and again and noted that the penis has not lost its capacity for erection, the illusion of damage is dissipated. Opportunities for repeated, unconflicted observation of adult sex are rare in Western culture, in which the concept of sexual privacy is well established. Even when children can see and hear what is going on in their parents' bed, families frequently maintain the myth that this is not so. Parents convince themselves that the children are "too young to understand," asleep, or disinterested. Children know that they are not supposed to be witnesses to the furtive acts left unshielded by the circumstances of necessity. Secrecy and prohibition, whether successful or not, add fuel to the flames of frightening sexual fantasies.

Without either the opportunity for unlimited observation or the possibility of socially acceptable sexual outlets for children, witnessing adult sex can be both overstimulating for children and evocative of scary misconceptions. But this is not always and necessarily the case. While parents usually prefer to avoid these times, children may sometimes wander in unannounced. These occasions are best handled without panic or guilt about wounded young psyches. Telling the child that you want to be left alone and that you will be available in a short time is usually sufficient for the time being. Later you can explain what you were doing and ask if the child has any questions. Hearing you speak of the love and pleasure of sex will help counteract any impression of violence. Clear, simple, and forthright answers to questions can give them the information they seek without compromising your own intimacy and comfort or overstimulating them.

Homosexuality

Janet's seven-year-old son came home one day and said: "Mom, some of the boys at school said if you like boys and you're a boy, then you're a faggot. And if you like girls and you're a girl, then you're a les. What does that mean?"

How could she give him a satisfactory answer to a question so layered with concern and value judgments? She knew he'd be gone in a minute, out of the house to play with his friends. She told him: "That's not an easy thing to answer, but it's true people have attitudes. Some people feel that it's not okay, and I don't think that's right. Everybody likes people who are the same sex as they are, and some people love people who are the same." Later that day she overheard him talking to a friend who had come over to spend the night. "You can't sleep in my bed with me," he told his friend. "Boys aren't supposed to love. I can like you but I can't love you." And Janet felt sad that his emotional world was narrowing.

Janet's point of view is far less common than Gene's. Gene had forbidden Carol to buy their son a doll, despite repeated requests by four-year-old Alan. No son of his was going to be a sissy! Playing with dolls at four was only the first step down the road to adult deviance. Better to avoid that first step than try to reverse a trend further down the line. Like other parents who anxiously hover over children who make the "wrong" choices for their gender, Gene's message to Alan is "There's something wrong with your wanting a doll, so there's something wrong with you."

A joke that made the rounds several years ago parodied the popular belief that overbearing mothers produced homosexual sons. One man is complaining to another, "Mother made me a homosexual." His friend replies, "If I'm real nice to her, will she make me one?" Despite theory and countertheory about the family constellations that lead to adult homosexuality, there does not seem to be a standard recipe. Some theorists claim that dominating mothers and passive fathers lead to deviant sons, while others blame passive mothers and bullying fathers. All we seem to know at the present time is that we don't know for sure what childhood factors influence adults to choose a homosexual life style. When asked by parents, this question is more a self-blaming "Where did we go wrong?" that also condemns the child than a disinterested scientific inquiry into how human beings choose their sexual partners.

One thing we do know is that deviating from sex-role norms is not evidence of "latent homosexuality." Children who follow their own interest patterns, rather than toeing the line of stereotypically appropriate behavior, are more likely to be imaginative and creative than in need of guidance. In the last decade we have begun to pay more attention to where our attitudes come from about what behaviors, interests, and abilities are uniquely male or female. Few of the differences we have come to expect between the sexes are actually innately determined. Because we will never have a culture-free environment in which to raise children, we will probably never be able to definitely assess how much of "feminine" or "masculine" behavior is the product of social conditions and how much is "natural." The best we can do is support the choices children make for themselves, letting them know that who they are is all right with us.

Growing up usually involves some experimenting with roles and relationships. Sex play typically occurs with members of the same sex as well as between the sexes. Best friends of the same sex are often the most important person outside the family for older children. "Crushes" on older people of the same sex are common among preadolescents and early teenagers. In this way, young people find someone outside the family whom they want to emulate at a time when they have a real need for other than parental models. All these attachments, which can be very intense, are a natural part of growing up. Parents can be helpful to their growing children by being there to discuss concerns as they arise.

Sol Gordon defines a homosexual as an adult who prefers and has sexual relations with members of the same sex. There is no such thing as a homosexual child. Or a heterosexual child. The choice of a predominantly homosexual or heterosexual life style is not made until the individual is a sexually active adult or adolescent. Nor is the initial choice necessarily permanent. People who have led "straight" lives for years, complete with marriage and children, later choose to be "gay." And vice versa.

Many parents are genuinely distressed to find that their grown children are leading homosexual life styles. It is frequently difficult for parents when children make choices radically different from their own, especially about something as central as a sexual partner. They want reassurance that the way they have lived their lives is valid and worthwhile and that their choices have been good for their children.

When children make very different choices for themselves, parents can experience this as a personal rebuke rather than the self-determination of a separate person.

In 1973 the American Psychiatric Association removed homosexuality from its list of pathological conditions. Although no longer officially considered "sick," homosexuals still suffer from their rejection by a society that discounts them on the basis of their sexual preference. What can hurt most, however, is being rejected by one's parents. Sometimes parents may think that withholding acceptance of a son's or daughter's life style may serve as a wedge to pry their child loose from that life choice. This vindictive "making it harder" seldom accomplishes its goal, but simply makes the hurt and anger on both sides more intense. Parents can communicate their disappointment and pain to their children without blaming them or trying to change them. Permission to talk about any subject and to bring friends home keeps channels of communication and contact open. "I don't like your choice, but I love you and I won't try to change you" is enough of an affirmation to build a mutually supportive relationship. Talking with other parents whose children are homosexual, sharing their disappointment and frustration and learning from one another how to weather the transition in expectations, has helped many parents strengthen endangered family ties.

Increased social tolerance is not the cause of more open homosexuality, but rather its result. Attitudes change when material conditions change. When the commandment "Be fruitful and multiply" echoed through the land, the social cost of homosexuality was too prohibitive for it to be condoned. Now, with real concern about the ability of the earth to support a rapidly multiplying population, society can afford to have some of its number choose not to make reproductive pairings.

It was easier for children to learn about the world when there was less diversity in adult roles and behavior—as it is easier for children to learn about the world when the adult community shares a common set of values about life, love, and childrearing. But, easier or not, that doesn't seem to describe contemporary urban America. Pretending that complexity doesn't exist won't make it go away.

Heterosexual parents will be called upon to explain homosexuality to their children. To help them avoid conflicts about their own behavior and friendships, parents would do well to explain both homosexuality and heterosexuality as including sexual relations and not just who loves whom, arguing for a more expansive definition of love than who beds with whom. It is helpful for parents to admit their prejudices, when and where they have them. If they are disapproving of homosexuality, explicitness about the social value system gives their children needed information: "Yes, the world is like that." Liberal parents who ignore their own prejudice and that of others only mystify their children about social reality.

Homosexual parents have a harder time of it. Because the community doesn't acknowledge their existence, they are invisible, and their children become invisible, too. Their special needs are neglected by social institutions. Cultural categories do not include their experience, making it more difficult for these parents to present a clear and accurate picture of their lives and others' to their children.

The four-year-old daughter of a lesbian came to nursery school and asked each of her teachers, "Do you have a boyfriend?" If the answer was "Yes," she probed further: "Is it a boy or a girl?" She knew from the world outside her home, with the television its resident ambassador, that a "boyfriend" is the sexual-romantic role in relationship to a woman. At home she learned that this role could be filled by another woman. Her investigations at school were part of an anthropological exploration of the culture she was attempting to get to know as a native. Being able to talk about these questions was vital to her overcoming the oppressive silence about her kind of family that greeted her whenever she left the house. A child cannot feel invisible and still come to know and value herself.

Although far more prepared for their children not to follow in their footsteps, homosexual parents, like any parents, can feel betrayed when their children make different choices from theirs. Like any parents, they learn that having children does not mean reproducing themselves. Bringing children into the world, parents create new people, whom they can influence but whose choices they cannot control.

Adoption

Talking with adopted children about how people get babies adds another issue to be explained. In addition to the mechanics of sex and birth, the child needs to know why her mommy and daddy are not the people who "growed" her. Most adoptive parents recognize the importance of telling their children how much they were wanted and how happy their parents were when they finally came to live with them. But even children confident of their parents' love may wonder why their biological mother (and father) gave them up. Was there something wrong with the child that he could be discarded? Children can use their parents' help in assuring them that they are valuable and welcome. But assurance is more persuasive if some of the negative fantasies of rejection and unworthiness are exposed to the light and revealed to be unconvincing. Here again the dialogue format of presenting information is the most persuasive, allowing children to air their concerns and let their parents know what it is they need in the way of information and support.

"Why did that mommy give me away?" asked Eli.

"Why do you think, Eli?" his mother replied.

"I guess she didn't like me. Maybe I was naughty."

"Well, she really didn't have time to find out what you were like, Eli. She probably decided she couldn't keep you before you were born, when she didn't know anything about you. She didn't even know if you were a boy or a girl. Maybe she never even saw you. I think there must be another reason. Can you think what it might be?"

"No."

"Well, I think it was because she couldn't take care of you the way she wanted you to be taken care of. Maybe she wasn't even all grown up yet. Sometimes people start babies when they weren't planning to make a baby. Maybe the woman who gave birth to you wasn't able to take care of a baby. Maybe she was still too young to make a good home for you. And she knew that there are people who want a baby very much, people who don't have a baby but want to love and take care of a baby. And even though she didn't know you yet, she loved you enough to want you to have the best care you could have. And I'm very happy that she did, because it makes me feel real glad that I'm your Mommy [or Daddy]."

Even children who are not adopted want and need to understand adoption. Most children wonder at one time or another if they were adopted, once they learn that others are. They want to understand how someone might choose to relinquish a child born to her, and they need to be reassured that they will not be given away, even if they are not always well behaved. They wonder why people cannot bear children if they want them, and they may want to know what can go wrong in the process of sex and conception to make a couple unable to reproduce. But childlessness is not the only reason for adoption, nor should it be the only explanation. People who love children and want another child in their lives can also choose not to bring a new baby into the world when they can share their love and their home with a child who already exists and needs a family.

Bibliography

Barbach, Lonnie Garfield. *For Yourself: the Fulfillment of Female Sexuality*. New York: Doubleday and Company, 1975.

Fraiberg, Selma H. *The Magic Years: Understanding and Handling the Problems of Early Childhood*. New York: Charles Scribner's Sons, 1959.

Freud, Sigmund. "On the Sexual Theories of Children." (1908) In *The Collected Papers of Sigmund Freud*. Edited by Philip Rieff. New York: Collier Books, 1963.

Gadpaille, Warren J. *The Cycles of Sex*. Edited by Lucy Freeman. New York: Charles Scribner's Sons, 1975.

Gordon, Sol. *Let's Make Sex a Household Word: a Guide for Parents and Children*. New York: John Day Company, 1975.

Kagan, Jerome. *Understanding Children: Behavior, motives and thought*. New York: Harcourt Brace Jovanovich, Inc., 1971.

Kohlberg, Lawrence. *Stages in the Development of Moral Thought and Action*. New York: Holt, Rinehart and Winston, 1969.

Laurendeau, M., and A. Pinard. *Causal Thinking in the Child*. New York: International Universities Press, 1962.

Lemke, Sonne. "Identity and Conservation: the Child's Developing Conceptions of Social and Physical Transformation." Unpublished doctoral dissertation, University of California, Berkeley, 1973.

Piaget, Jean. *The Child's Conception of the World*. Totowa, New Jersey: Littlefield, Adams and Company, 1975.

Piaget, Jean. *The Child's Conception of Physical Causality*. Totowa, New Jersey: Littlefield, Adams and Company, 1975.

Piaget, Jean. *Judgment and Reasoning in the Child*. Totowa, New Jersey: Littlefield, Adams and Company, 1968.

Piaget, Jean and Barbel Inhelder. *The Psychology of the Child.* New York: Basic Books, 1960.

Pomeroy, Wardell B. *Your Child and Sex: a Guide for Parents.* New York: Dell Publishing Company, 1974.

Turiel, Eliot. "Developmental Processes in the Child's Moral Thinking." In *New Directions in Developmental Psychology.* Edited by P. Mussen, J. Langer and M. Covinton. New York: Holt, Rinehart and Winston, 1969.